ACHIEVING
BS EN ISO 9000

THE SUNDAY TIMES BUSINESS SKILLS SERIES

"excellent ... well worth reading"

Christopher Lorenz, the *Financial Times*

The Sunday Times Business Skills Series is an up-to-the-minute collection of books covering essential management topics in the three key areas of total quality management, personal skills and leadership skills.

Combining current management theory and practice with detailed case examples and practical advice, each book provides a definitive stand-alone summary of best management practice in a specific field.

Books already published in the series:

PERFORMANCE APPRAISALS
Martin Fisher
ISBN 0 7494 2021 9 (Paperback)
ISBN 0 7494 1441 3 (Hardback)

BUILDING YOUR TEAM
Rupert Eales-White
ISBN 0 7494 2019 7 (Paperback)
ISBN 0 7494 1342 5 (Hardback)

MANAGING CHANGE
Philip Sadler
ISBN 0 7494 2022 7 (Paperback)
ISBN 0 7494 1343 3 (Hardback)

ACHIEVING BS EN ISO 9000
Peter Jackson and David Ashton
ISBN 0 7494 2023 5 (Paperback)
ISBN 0 7494 1440 5 (Hardback)

EFFECTIVE NEGOTIATING
Colin Robinson
ISBN 0 7494 2020 0 (Paperback)

The Sunday Times Business Skills series comprises not only a range of books, but also a comprehensive series of video-based training courses.

Produced by Taylor Made Films, these highly acclaimed courses provide invaluable information on particular subjects and are flexible and easy to use.

Each course contains everything you need to learn about the subject. There are two videos, the first of which dramatises the key messages and the second shows how British organisations have put the key issues into practice. The videos are accompanied by a self-study workbook, or a course leader's guide.

There are currently fifteen courses in the series. For more information or a catalogue, please contact Taylor Made Films on 01264 335577.

ACHIEVING
BS EN ISO 9000

Peter Jackson
and David Ashton

KOGAN
PAGE

First published in 1995
Paperback edition published in 1996

Kogan Page Limited
120 Pentonville Road
London N1 9JN

© Peter Jackson and David Ashton, 1995, 1996

British Library Cataloguing in Publication Data

A CIP record for this book is available from the British Library.

ISBN 0 7494 1440 5 (Hardback) ISBN 0 7494 2023 5 (Paperback)

Typeset by Saxon Graphics Ltd, Derby
Printed in England by Clays Ltd, St Ives plc

Contents

Preface

The origin of this book was a real ISO 9000 project. One of us (Peter Jackson) had the job of achieving ISO 9000 for his company – Business & Market Research Plc – a first time registration for the market research industry, and the other (David Ashton) used his quality management expertise to advise as a consultant (working with Daisley Associates). One thing we recognised was a lack of a simple guide to what ISO 9000 was all about and how to achieve it. In time, this led us to write a book – *Implementing Quality Through BS 5750 (ISO 9000)*. Since then we are a bit older and hopefully a little wiser and have added, in this publication for the Sunday Times Business Skills Series, some additional ideas as well as including material from our more detailed first book. We have also taken account of changes made to ISO 9000 in the 1994 revision.

We hope our book will provide a clear idea of what ISO 9000 is all about and be a useful and practical guide to anyone given the responsibility of implementing the Standard.

Peter Jackson
David Ashton
September 1994

1

Introduction

The 1990s is the decade of quality. We need to hang on to sales in recession, but also be ready to expand and find new customers. The increasing competitiveness of business has brought home to managers that quality is not something extra, not something that is nice to have but something which is a condition for survival. Similar forces have had the same impact in public services and other non-commercial organisations. All sorts of approaches to achieving and keeping quality are recommended. Each has something to offer but the subject of this book is quality assurance and particularly systems to meet a recognised standard for quality management.

Until now the recognised standard for quality management, in the UK, has been known as BS 5750, although the European equivalent – EN 29000 – and the international ISO 9000 have also become increasingly familiar. In fact the three standards; BS 5750, EN 29000 and ISO 9000 were identical in content and a firm registered for one has been able to automatically claim the other two. In mid-1994, the British Standards Institution (BSI), revised its Standard in line with changes to ISO 9000. Generally these have been only minor shifts in emphasis and the most dramatic change has been in the title. BS 5750 is no more. The new and full name adopted is BS EN ISO 9000.[1] Possibly this will catch on in management speak but we doubt it and think it more likely that ISO 9000 will be the common way of referring to it. Throughout this book, therefore, except where we provide a little

---

[1] The letters relate the Standard to its national, European and international origins.

history (Chapter 2) we stick to using ISO 9000 (or for variety 'the Standard'). We even use ISO 9000 when discussing case histories of firms which gained the Standard as 'BS 5750'.

Whatever it is called, ISO 9000 has taken off in the UK to a remarkable extent. In many cases, this is because firms believe that a systematic approach to quality, which is the basis of the Standard, is an effective management tool for achieving quality goals. However, there can be no doubt that there is also a band-wagon effect and many managers have more or less felt forced to seek an ISO 9000 certificate. In turn they may push others – their suppliers – along the same route. Why shouldn't they suffer as well! We think it a pity if a firm has to 'do' ISO 9000; coercion is not the best starting point for quality. However, whatever the reason for considering ISO 9000 may be, our first purpose in this book is to provide a straightforward guide to the Standard and what it really requires. With that knowledge, we hope that a better informed decision can be made on whether to go for ISO 9000. This then leads into our second aim; to give a guide on *how* to do it – to be successfully assessed to the Standard.

Chapters 2 to 7 cover our first aim of providing an understanding of ISO 9000. As background, a little quality philosophy is needed and this, together with a short history of ISO 9000, is provided in Chapters 2 and 3. With these basic concepts we then discuss the major benefits that implementing the Standard can bring. But there are potential problems and downsides as well, and in this chapter, we also cover the case against this route to quality. Some more detailed aspects of ISO 9000 are then examined in Chapter 4 including an overview of the requirements of the Standard. We think it useful (and no more than that) to discuss these requirements in three groupings linked to an organisation's activities, rather than in the order in which they are set out in the published standard. These are covered in Chapters 5 (ISO 9000 requirements to meet in the firm's operating processes), 6 (support activities) and 7 (controlling the quality system itself). Hopefully, these chapters will give someone new to the subject a feeling for what has to be done, in practice, to meet and gain the Standard. However, and we shall repeat this warning later, our commentary (or anyone else's) should be regarded as an adjunct to and not an alternative to reading the published standard itself. Assessment is against the Standard and definitely not against our book.

Chapters 8 to 11 then provide some guidance on how to achieve ISO 9000. This standard is based on a documented quality system and what is needed in this respect is discussed in Chapter 8. Some examples of the documents are provided. Chapter 9 is about how to develop such a system and with a stress on staff involvement; not just as a means to an effective system but also as part of a more overall quality stance. Preparing the necessary documents and procedures is the bulk of the initial work needed to gain ISO 9000, but a system is certainly not just literature. It must be made to work effectively – be implemented – and this is the subject of Chapter 10. Chapter 11 then takes the whole project to at least its initial goal – successful assessment by a recognised body.

Chapter 12 goes back to more general principles with a discussion of what might come after ISO 9000 for a business which recognises the essential truth that quality is a process and ongoing. In particular, we show how some of the things which have to be done to gain the ISO 9000 certificate can be usefully and effectively extended.

Throughout the book we illustrate many of our points by examples from some real case studies. These are all organisations featured in one of the videos of the Sunday Times Business Skills pack. Briefly, these are as follows:

Benfell Communications. This small company, based in Blackpool, supplies and installs communication, security and audio equipment for vehicles. The range is extensive and back-up support to customers is a cornerstone of the business. It holds a dealership from Vodac and was encouraged by this major player in the market to seek ISO 9000 (Vodac now requires all its dealers to be registered to the Standard).

Datac Adhesives. With over 500 adhesive products marketed internationally, Datac Adhesives is a major producer in its industry. Gaining ISO 9000 was part of its commitment to the highest product and service quality and a means to improve control of the processes involved.

P&O European Ferries. This company is the leading UK cross-channel operator. The business is complex, with revenue and profits gained through a mix of activities including on-board catering, duty free sales as well as the ferry operation itself. P&O has an overall quality programme 'The Standard of Excellence', and this brings together a number of management tools. ISO 9000 was considered to be an effective means of implementing quality management systems.

DHL International (UK). This company is part of the world-wide DHL Group offering air express delivery in over 200 countries. DHL International (UK) operates from sites across the country and has gained ISO 9000 for its whole operation. Like many successful companies, DHL regards quality systems as an important but not sole part of an overall commitment to and programme for quality improvement.

Kent County Council Highways And Transportation. Road development and construction work is at a high level in Kent and is managed, alongside other transport matters, by this department of the County Council. It was one of the first local authority and public service operations to gain an ISO 9000 certificate.

Park Farm. In having ISO 9000, Park Farm is very unusual if not unique. One reason for this approach is that farming is a second career for John Axon, who had valued quality assurance and the Standard when he ran an engineering factory. He believed that systematic methods could also work on the farm he had bought and worked with his wife Diane for some 17 years. It is now a successful venture producing quality beef on 150 acres in Warwickshire.

The case studies are, therefore, very varied in the activities carried out, their scope and organisational size. However, as we shall show, ISO 9000 is potentially a practical approach for almost any operation.

2

What is ISO 9000?

ISO 9000 is a standard for quality assurance. To understand what this means we need to start with the concept of quality. We can then discuss how quality is achieved and maintained in business and the value of the quality assurance approach.

QUALITY – MEETING REQUIREMENTS

In normal language, quality is often linked to an idea of excellence. High quality products are the 'top of the market', invariably the most expensive and exclusive – supplied by specialists for the very few. What makes them high quality may not be obvious apart from their price, where they are sold and probably their brand name. Used in this sense, quality in the business world is for specialists catering for niche markets and is little use for those selling at competitive prices in the mass market. It is also of limited use in technical businesses where the customers' requirements are specified in terms of physical properties and leave little room for an intangible and unmeasurable excellence.

The concept of quality underlying ISO 9000 is of *meeting requirements*. A product or service, therefore, has quality when it satisfies the needs of users – it meets customer requirements. For any business which depends for its ultimate survival on satisfying a market (and all have to), meeting customer requirements is clearly vital. If customers are not satisfied they can always buy from someone else. In this sense, therefore, quality is *the* core task of a business; it is not an option – it is essential for survival.

The need to meet requirements can also be extended to public services. These have a duty to serve their communities efficiently. The penalties for a failure to meet needs may be less immediate but none the less real. Kent County Council Highways and Transportation for example recognises its duty to deliver value for money as part of its public service and this is bound up with the concept of meeting requirements in road maintenance.

Although quality, as meeting requirements, rightly focuses first and foremost on customers (or the public), there are also intermediate requirements that must be met within the organisation if the customer is to be ultimately satisfied. If Datac's adhesive products are to meet their customers' needs the purchasing department must ensure that the plant is supplied with materials which are appropriate. P&O European Ferries' on-board restaurants can only satisfy their customers if the food is to an adequate quality; so that the chefs can cook appetising dishes. Quality as meeting requirements is, therefore, a concern throughout an organisation and not just a matter for the sales force or other departments with direct customer contact. A vision of an organisation consisting of chains of internal customers and suppliers, leading ultimately to satisfying the final customer, can be very effective in ensuring that a commitment to quality is shared throughout an organisation.

Finally, there is another important group whose requirements must be met by a business – the owners or shareholders who demand a return on their investment – a profit must be made. In a public service the equivalent is value for money or minimising the burden on the taxpayer. This requires that customer requirements must be met and quality delivered at least-cost and, therefore, in the most efficient way. In turn this will tend to drive down the prices in a market and enhance customer satisfaction.

MEETING ALL REQUIREMENTS

Few will argue with the idea that businesses at least should or have to meet their customers' requirements. Of course they must

– why make a big issue (or write books) about the obvious? However, although it is all so obvious it is not hard to find examples of businesses which do not meet customers' needs; or at least do not do so all the time. Quite possibly the average buyer (whether domestic or working professionally) finds that in most transactions some of his or her requirements, including the seemingly trivial, are not fully met; the food in the restaurant was all right but the waiter's attitude left something to be desired, the delivery got there but the information given on the phone was confusing, or the mobile phone worked but the instruction leaflet was a puzzle. The point is that customer requirements are nearly always complex with many components and in practice it can be a major task to identify what these are and very difficult to satisfy them for all customers all of the time. Yet the company who can do so, or come closest, will have the competitive advantage. Attention to all the details of requirements and therefore quality is, consequently, by no means a trivial matter and, on the contrary, should be at the core of a company's mission (whether or not this is expressed in the now fashionable mission statements). In the end, neglect of quality always leads to the same result – business failure; it is not hard to find examples of those who fundamentally failed to meet their customers' requirements.

One aspect of the complexity of achieving quality is that meeting customer requirements involves both *implicit and explicit* requirements. When customers book with P&O European Ferries, the apparent and explicit requirement is to take them and their vehicles from Dover to Calais or on other routes within the advertised times. However, there are other needs, which although not specified in the terms and conditions of the ticket sale are also very important to customers – they probably want to relax for an hour or so before continuing their car journey, they may wish to enjoy a meal or use the many other services offered on-board, and above all there is an implicit requirement to be carried safely. The latter, in turn, requires all sorts of things to be done of which passengers may be quite unaware. Meeting customer needs, therefore, requires a detailed analysis and under-

17

standing of these needs and often carrying out work which is hidden from customers' view. Sometimes meeting one need may involve conflict with others – passengers may like to have access to their vehicles throughout the voyage but safety considerations preclude this.

Attention to customer needs nearly always involves meeting technical performance criteria in a product or service and in this context quality is sometimes referred to as *fit for purpose*. Whatever else, Datac's adhesives must meet their customers' requirements for secure bonding; if the things meant to be stuck together come apart, customers' requirements are not being met. Rightly, companies supplying technical products (often to other businesses – to industrial markets) put considerable emphasis behind meeting requirements of this sort through quality inspection and control and in their research and development programmes which anticipate customers' future needs. Quality also involves recognising that requirements are not fixed forever but constantly change and, with the pace of technical innovation, at an ever increasing rate.

However, meeting requirements and therefore offering quality does not end at providing a technically satisfactory product or service. Other aspects of customer requirements need to be recognised and technically orientated companies often place insufficient emphasis in these areas. These include design in the aesthetic sense – other things being equal the product that looks 'right' will be preferred over another with comparable technical features – and possibly packaging. There are in addition all the aspects of meeting customer requirements that come under the umbrella of service. This includes the more obvious things such as delivery of products in good condition and on time as well as the manner in which enquiries and orders are handled – DHL International for example puts considerable stress in training reservations staff – giving back-up maintenance support and even recognising the need to handle complaints efficiently and well.

Complaint handling leads to a final aspect of quality; the ability of an organisation to solve problems arising from failures in meeting requirements. In this sense, quality leads to a reduction of wasteful and costly mistakes. Not only can quality be afforded and not only must it be afforded, it should have no net cost since achieving it saves waste and adds value (see also Chapter 3).

DELIGHTING CUSTOMERS

In the fullest sense, meeting customer requirements is a complex matter and not only is this all that needs to be done, it is all that can be done in relation to customers – if they are fully satisfied what else can we offer them? Some consider it useful to think of 'delighting' customers as well. If we 'just' meet customers' needs they will be satisfied but if we go one step further, perhaps give them something which they can recognise as valuable but unexpected and perhaps something they did not even know they wanted, they will be more than satisfied – they will be delighted. Not only will they buy again they will be loath to even consider anyone else.

The concept of delighting customers leads into Total Quality Management (TQM) which is often considered a step beyond what can be achieved by putting in an effective quality system such as to ISO 9000 (see also Chapter 12). However, the difference between fully meeting customer requirements and delighting them, is in practice slight; possibly more semantic than real.

GETTING AND KEEPING QUALITY

The identification of customer needs is a vital aspect of quality, involving keeping close to your customer base and often carrying out formal market research. Assuming that we know what customers require, how are we to ensure that it is provided? How do we get quality and how do we keep it consistently and constantly?

The traditional approach has been to focus on the final product. A regime of quality inspection is set up to determine whether the product coming out of the workplace or process matches up to requirements. This involves testing the product, inspecting it and probably measuring various technical parameters. Whether or not they are given the title, the work is carried out by quality inspectors, usually at the end of the process (final inspection) and before the product is shipped off to customers. The work of inspection may involve all products or controlled samples, an aspect of the technique known as statistical process control (SPC).

Quality inspection necessarily involves some specification of what the product's characteristics ought to be. This needs to be in writing and include a methodology for the tests with acceptable ranges of test results – products with measurements outside this range are classified as rejects and sent for scrap or remedial work. The specification may be original to the producer involved, although will normally involve some element of agreed customer requirements and where appropriate, will take account of any regulations affecting the product (eg those relating to safety). However, within an industry, it is usually convenient to adopt some common technical standards for products and define these as recognised standards for the product – product approval specifications (PAS). These ensure the product is at least minimally fit for its purpose and provides a basic common framework for buyer and seller. Both may agree that a particular order should have additional features over and above the common PAS, but by incorporating this recognised standard, both buyer and seller avoid much work and the possibility of disagreement in establishing agreed technical specifications. In some markets products are specified in terms of such a PAS alone and at least in a technical sense, any supplier meeting this is meeting customer requirements.

There are various routes to PASs but the best known and established in the UK are the specifications published by the British Standard Institution. Such BSs exist and are used throughout British industry and abroad. Virtually every physical product has a relevant BS (eg BS 1449 – a standard for stainless steel tube) and they (or other PASs) are also found in services, although, since they consist of technical specifications which are objectively measurable, this approach may be less applicable in activities with a low product content – eg professional services such as the law.

The inspection approach to quality is very well established and at least in the case of technical products, is usually essential to some degree, regardless of any other methods used as well. However, in isolation, quality inspection has at least two major limitations. Firstly, the activities of the quality inspector start only once the product is complete – he stands away from production and concerns himself only with passing or failing whatever comes out of this process; what happens there is of no concern to him. The quality inspector's performance measure is rejection rates and arguably the higher this is the better his performance. However, rejection is a failure within the factory and to accept a given rate of rejection is to institutionalise waste, whose costs are not only the material element being scrapped but also the manufacturing time and effort that has gone into the faulty product. If the only quality control methodology is final inspection, carried out outside the production process, the causes of defects will never be found nor waste levels reduced.

There is also another serious limitation to a sole reliance on inspection. This is that some qualities of a product, and even more so of a service, cannot be adequately tested after production. Defects either cannot practically or in principle be measured before delivery to the customer. DHL International's customers require their packages to be delivered on time and in good condition. This cannot be established until the service is complete and, therefore, after any shortfall is translated into customer dissatisfaction. Defects identified after production are bad enough but at least with physical products the additional costs – and very real and serious costs – of dissatisfied customers is not incurred as well. In the case of delivery services and similar businesses, defects can be measured only *after* the event and in other service businesses even this cannot be done. In a professional service *how* and *who* carries out the work is a vital aspect of quality and not

how much have BA saved companies

apparent in the final 'delivery'. A client requesting legal advice relies on his solicitor to take due care and diligence and is in no position to test that advice once given.

In practice, few businesses rely solely on final inspection to maintain quality although many still put too much emphasis on this approach. Usually failures are related to the production process and adjustments are made to address the obvious causes of scrap. This may involve setting parameters for the operation of plant and carrying out intermediate as well as final quality inspection, so that defects can be related to the immediately preceding process. Such *quality control* methods are an attempt to overcome the limitations of a sole reliance on final quality inspection. However, what both have in common is a focus on the products and their characteristics – in other words *what* is produced. *Quality assurance* is a radically different approach to quality and moves attention from what is produced to *how* it is produced.

QUALITY ASSURANCE

Underlying quality assurance is the idea that right methods will either produce right results (quality products) or at least be more likely to do so. Quality assurance, therefore, involves the planning and management of all activities with any bearing on the quality of the final output. These are most of the things which happen within a business organisation. This approach to quality is very much concerned with minimising defects – to stop rejects being produced – and, therefore, it is directly concerned with increasing efficiency (which quality inspection ignores). With effective quality assurance, the reduced opportunity to produce defects should reduce the need for inspection and arguably the goal might be to do without inspection entirely; or at least after-the-event inspection. In practice, however, quality assurance and some level of inspection are usually regarded as complementary approaches to achieving quality and ISO 9000, which is a standard for quality assurance, requires inspection activities to be part of the approach to maintaining quality.

Quality assurance assumes that at a given time, in given circumstances, there is one best way to carry out each major step in a process and that adherence to this method will minimise defects and quality problems. Since all activities relevant to quality are addressed, these defined best ways of working can be regarded as making up a system – a *quality system*.

QUALITY SYSTEMS

In a small business an effective quality system may be informal and undocumented. Through working closely together, the staff know how the job should be done to produce the best results and have no need to consult records. However, even in the smallest business a purely informal and unwritten system can lead to problems. What happens in the uncommon cases? How should the work be done if customer needs change and what happens if a new member of staff is brought in? Sooner or later, at least parts of the system need to be written down, if only haphazardly. However, as time goes on, these too become out of date or it is uncertain which of a series of several notes now applies. When this stage is reached it may be time to have a structured system, set out in a formal quality or procedure manual, and to which everyone works.

In the move from informal to formal quality systems there are dangers, particularly in retaining flexibility and the ability to react to a changing environment. A formal system must strike a balance between specifying how key tasks are to be carried out and going to such detail that requirements slightly deviating from the normal cannot be accommodated – a quality system must never hinder meeting customer requirements. Similarly, no matter how well thought through, a quality system must have a built-in facility to adapt to such changes as a structural shift in customer demand and the technologies available for meeting these needs. Anybody planning a quality system must consider these needs for balance and flexibility.

Even within an industry, let alone between different types of businesses, an effective quality system will be unique. The methods of working which are best for Datac, in the adhesive business, will cover very different concerns to what DHL International consider important in the courier business and, in detail, DHL methods of work will be different to their direct competitors. However, despite these major differences, all effective quality systems can be related to some general principles. These are discussed at length elsewhere in this book (especially Chapters 4 to 7) but two examples are process control and traceability. All businesses can be seen as a process – a series of steps – and although it may seem bizarre, this applies as much to a professional service as 'process' manufacturing such as in the chemical industry. In all cases, something is carried out after something precedes it (the input) and then something follows (the output) until the final product comes out. Defining these steps – these chains of inputs, process and output – is process control. Similarly, in all types of business, faults should be traced back to the cause of the problem – the principle of traceability – so that they can be corrected or compensation sought from a supplier (Datac have found this a very effective aspect of a quality system).

Taken together, such principles which can be applied to a quality system are another sort of specification – a specification for the *capability* of a business to manage quality activities. ISO 9000 is the most widely recognised such specification.

THE ORIGINS OF ISO 9000

The origins of ISO 9000 lie in wartime and the defence industry. The problem of defects in ammunition and the need for reliability in equipment on which survival might depend, moved the focus to controlling how the work was done. Eventually this led to defined standards (eg Defence Standard 05-21) for quality management to which defence contractors were expected to work. As the concept of quality management and quality systems became known, buyers in non-defence industries started to demand that their own suppliers of technical products adopt quality systems. For reasons which will be mentioned shortly, it proved desirable to have a common standard for quality systems which could be applied to any industry and in 1979 this led the BSI to publish a first version of BS 5750 (revised in 1987 and 1994). A similar need for a quality system arose in many other countries and BS 5750 was taken as a model for other national standards. Eventually common European (EN 29000) and international (ISO 9000) standards were prepared and this process has now come full circle with the international standard (effectively the British Standard) for quality management re-titled BS EN ISO 9000 in the 1994 revision.

THE APPLICATION OF ISO 9000 TO ALL BUSINESSES

Anyone reading ISO 9000 for the first time, and especially someone who is not from an engineering type business, may find it obscure and difficult. Many of the assumptions underlying it assume a certain type of process is carried out and it is often difficult to relate this to quite different types of businesses. The taunt that the Standard was 'written by engineers for engineers' is not without some foundation. However, the principles of quality management can be followed in any business and with interpretation, the requirements in ISO 9000 can be applied in all circumstances. In the rest of this book this contention of universal application will be amplified. However, the uptake of ISO 9000 is such that it is also demonstrated empirically – there are now few types of businesses without some firms registered to the Standard. The range of companies used in this book as case studies is an illustration of this. Also the approach to quality on which the Standard is based has been adopted by a wide spread of non-business organisations (eg schools, medical practices, local government), some of whom have gone the whole way to ISO 9000 registration although for various reasons others have decided this to be inappropriate (eg the Metropolitan Police have adopted a quality system but have not sought assessment to the Standard).

TWO MISCONCEPTIONS

There are two common misconceptions about ISO 9000 which can lead to serious misunderstanding and result in companies adopting or rejecting it for quite wrong reasons. The first misconception is the Standard is itself a quality system – it lays down how a company should be managed to enhance quality. This is untrue and in a sense obviously so; how can a short document be applied to every possible business? But on this basis, some write off ISO 9000 as 'meaningless' or 'not applicable in our type of business'. The Standard is no more than a set of principles – a template or framework – on which a unique quality system, to meet the needs of an individual organisation, can be based. Indeed the first priority of anyone planning a quality system must be the unique needs of their business, and meeting the requirements of ISO 9000 should be a secondary and almost incidental concern. A quality system which is well thought out and complete should largely match up to the Standard anyway.

The second common misconception is that ISO 9000 provides customers and others with some guarantee of product quality. Sometimes examples of false advertising claims in this respect can be found – eg a window supplier claiming 'all windows made to BS 5750'.

As such, the Standard says nothing about the particular quality of the product – in the sense of quality as excellence it may be high or low. ISO 9000 instead is a statement about how quality is managed and one implication of this is that the products are constantly made to consistent standards *whatever these standards are*. It is, therefore, quite possible that a customer may choose not to buy from an ISO 9000 registered company for the very good reason that the products are not to the right quality – they do not meet his requirements. To benefit his business the supplier may need to upgrade the technical or other standards of work to bring it into line with requirements. However, the benefit of ISO 9000 is that the quality system in place should ensure that the new product standards are effectively introduced and applied effectively. Consistency of this sort is important in almost all businesses and especially where the product of a supplier is the input into another's own process – it is no good finding Monday's batch of adhesive excellent but Wednesday's deficient. In summary, therefore, ISO 9000 is a standard for managing a quality *company* rather than a standard for a product.

In professional service businesses, the confusion about quality of product sometimes leads to the misunderstanding that ISO 9000 attempts to define or improve the quality level of the client service. This is not the case. The Standard simply does not relate to the quality of intellectual effort required to produce a high level of service – the consultant may follow all the steps in the process correctly, but still produce inappropriate conclusions if his or her thinking is poor. However, ISO 9000 will ensure that due care has been exercised in working methods and that the skills of staff and their training is taken into account before assigning them to a particular project.

ASSESSMENT

No matter whether a product or a capability and management standard is involved, it must be capable of being assessed. We or our customers must have a means of knowing whether or not we are working to whatever standard we claim.

Self or first party assessment involves us in devising and following a method to determine whether or not we are complying. Day to day this is a very important aspect of working to a standard but our customers may well wish to have some additional reassurance that we do what we say – work to the standard claimed. They may wish, therefore, to carry out their own, second party, assessment. In the case of a product standard this may be largely a matter of physically testing samples of goods delivered. If, however, the buyer is concerned that an adequate quality system is in place, second party assessment will involve visiting and carrying out an assessment at the supplier's premises. This is a nuisance to both supplier and customer. If the supplier has several customers, each demanding to assess the quality system, the whole thing can rapidly get out of hand with staff having to be employed just to deal with customer assessments. The need to avoid this was one of the impetuses to the development of BS 5750 – a published standard which could be assessed by third party or independent assessors. The bodies offering this service such as BSI QA, SGS Yarsley, Lloyds and NQA (to name only a few) are recognised as capable of carrying out objective and thorough assessments of quality systems[1] and, moreover, are approved by an official body – the United Kingdom Accreditation Service (UKAS).

GAINING ISO 9000 AND COMMITMENT TO QUALITY

In the barest outline (to be much expanded in later chapters) the process of gaining ISO 9000 is: design a quality system which meets the requirements of the Standard (and meets the needs of the individual firm), implement that system – make sure everyone involved is working to it – and then have a UKAS approved body[2] assess the system. Providing the assessors consider the system is in conformity with the Standard and they find that it is being followed, the certificate is then yours subject to periodic surveillance and re-assessment.

---

[1] These bodies are involved in other types of assessment work including to the environmental standard BS 7750. BSI QA are also involved in product certification through their Kitemark scheme. This involves product testing by the BSI but it should be noted that the Kitemark is only given to firms registered to BS/ISO 9000 – this is considered essential to guarantee that the product will be produced consistently to the product standard.

[2] An unapproved assessor can be used – anyone can set themselves up as assessors and award BS/ISO 9000. However, the value of such certification is unlikely to be recognised by customers or anyone else – see also Chapter 11.

As already explained, ISO 9000 can be applied and certification given to any type of business. In principle it can also be applied to any size of organisation regardless of the management structure. However, in all cases, one ingredient is essential; commitment. Firstly there must be commitment to developing an effective quality system. This will inevitably take considerable management time and require other significant expenditure. The commitment to the system, however, must also be on-going; it is not enough to design an effective system – it must also be implemented and followed all the time. Two things are conducive to this commitment; seeking ISO 9000 for good reasons and staff involvement. The former – the reasons for accreditation – is discussed in Chapter 3. Staff involvement is essential to both design an effective system and to obtain compliance in following it. A system imposed from above will be just that and never have more than token support from those who are meant to work it. Moreover, it will be a defective system because 'above' will certainly not adequately understand the processes to be controlled.

Commitment is also essential to achieve, keep and enhance quality. A system such as ISO 9000 will help to minimise quality problems and, if implemented effectively, have some in-built dynamic for quality improvement. However, it is only a tool and the people using it must have the right motivation and attitudes. The TQM approach (also considered in Chapter 12) is very much concerned with this human side to quality. But it is a complementary rather than an alternative approach to a quality system. DHL International, for example, sought ISO 9000 as part of an overall management commitment to total quality.

It is vital to recognise the link between quality systems and commitment to quality, which it is not only a one way relationship. Whilst commitment is needed to gain ISO 9000, the process of designing and implementing a quality system itself stimulates staff motivation to quality improvement. P&O European Ferries found this – involvement in achieving the Standard was a morale booster and it increased awareness of the need for the highest quality in customer service.

3

Is ISO 9000 Worth Having?

Developing a quality system and gaining ISO 9000 is a signifi-cant project for any organisation and it has a cost. What is the payback? This chapter looks at some of the benefits claimed for the Standard. It also considers potential problems and disadvan-tages of this approach.

CUSTOMER DEMAND

Though advocates of ISO 9000 may wish otherwise, many companies now going through the process of ISO 9000 are mainly doing so because they believe this is essential to keep vital business. They are doing it because major customers demand ISO 9000 from their suppliers or because it is feared that shortly they will insist on this evidence of quality assurance. P&O European Ferries, for example, were prompted to consider an ISO 9000 system by enquiries from freight customers (the decision to go ahead in this case was, however, taken for a number of reasons). Certainly customer demand for ISO 9000 exists – and, as a condition of approved supplier status, it is a formal policy of some major organisations. Some suppliers, particularly small ones, may realistically recognise that they have little choice but to seek registration to the Standard.

An equivalent demand is also found in other commercial rela-tionships including dealer networks. Benfell Communications, for example, was encouraged to seek ISO 9000 by Vodac and registration to the Standard is now demanded of all Vodac distributors. In the same market, BT is also strongly committed to ISO 9000 and demands it not only of suppliers but from authorised maintenance companies.

To help understand ISO 9000 and why it has been taken up widely, it is useful to consider the reasons some companies insist on or favour ISO 9000 supplier status. Almost always of course these companies have ISO 9000 themselves and believe that the approach offers some important advantages – not so much in terms of gaining business but in internal efficiency and managing quality effectively. Such companies may also believe that in turn their own suppliers are more likely to offer consistently high quality if they too follow similar principles in quality management. Furthermore, a quality system to ISO 9000 has requirements in terms of a need for formal supplier approval and evaluation. There is nothing in the Standard requiring that suppliers to an ISO 9000 company should be themselves registered to the Standard, but in practice, an ISO 9000-only supplier policy may become part of the purchasing system. This may be considered the most efficient method rather than the alternative of expensive and time consuming second party assessment, with the purchasing company's staff tied up in a never ending cycle of visits to suppliers. Nor are these benefits only one way. Suppliers also potentially gain from a decrease in assessment enquiries and visits and this may be a factor (along with others discussed below) to offset against the cost of ISO 9000 to meet customers' insistence.

ISO 9000 is also a convenient way for large company buyers to keep their supplier lists to manageable proportions. Every supplier in their field wants the valuable business of such large companies but a restricted range of close suppliers is generally considered to be more effective in the long run. Whether or not it is a thorough mechanism, an ISO 9000 policy automatically shortens the list of potential suppliers – by excluding the many who still have not gained the Standard.

Finally there is an issue of due diligence in choice of suppliers. Any future product liability cases may require a company to demonstrate that it has exercised due diligence in providing goods or services and this can extend to its purchasing policy and procedures. Whilst an ISO 9000-only supplier policy will not absolve a company from claims relating to choice of materials incorporated in their products, it may at least be a positive factor in any defence. Companies potentially facing claims of this sort (and almost all companies are at some risk) may consider ISO 9000 as a form of insurance.

ISO 9000-only supplier status and particularly where large companies impose it on small ones has led to adverse press coverage, with the Standard portrayed as the oppressive tool of bullies forcing well run small businesses to adopt an unsuitable set of 'bureaucratic' procedures just to stay in business. Without any doubt these stories exaggerate the position. ISO 9000 is a requirement in some markets and in some contracts but not to the extent that has been imagined. Misunderstandings happen. An enquiry by a customer about quality assurance may be treated as a demand for ISO 9000 when this was never intended. Also ISO 9000 can be a convenient scapegoat for lost business when the true cause lies elsewhere; uncompetitive prices, poor quality and indifferent service. The last two problems, however, might be overcome by a quality assurance approach.

Anyone considering ISO 9000 will almost certainly consider the extent to which customers are now or are likely in future to demand the Standard. The position will vary widely from industry to industry and most companies should be able to arrive at a judgement of the need in their own case. However, as we shall show, even if customer demand for the Standard is low, there may be other good reasons for considering a quality system to ISO 9000.

MARKETING BENEFITS

The marketing benefits of ISO 9000 can be thought of as the positive version of customer demand for the Standard. Customers may not (yet) ask for ISO 9000 from their suppliers but they may be impressed and more likely to do business with a supplier which can demonstrate a commitment to quality in this way. This is especially the case in industrial businesses where ISO 9000 is well known but it can even have some value in dealing with customers who have little idea of what the Standard is or what it means. In retail type businesses, customers are very unlikely to be even aware of ISO 9000 let alone of its implications. Even so, they may be vaguely impressed by 'the standard for quality'.

Gaining ISO 9000 may open up new business and particularly to smaller companies which gain the Standard. Large accounts, previously closed, become interested in doing business. This may be because having ISO 9000 is a formal condition of supply but more often it is a matter of perception – the supplier is seen to have 'raised the game' and to be serious about handling first-class business. The Standard is a public commitment to take quality issues seriously.

A real marketing advantage may also be gained by a company which is first in its own field to achieve ISO 9000. This lead may be short-term (as competitors are likely to follow suit) but could provide the vital step-up to a new level of accounts. This again may breach barriers to large accounts and make possible the growth of a smaller company. Also the 'pioneer' can use first in the field as some sort of special claim even when competitors have caught up.

ISO 9000 is an international standard, and this aspect may offer marketing advantages overseas. The uptake of ISO 9000 and its national equivalents (all developed countries have a national standard for quality assurance, broadly matching ISO 9000) is in fact much higher in the UK than elsewhere. However, in Europe and the US, interest and registration to such standards is growing and ISO 9000 can be used as a tool in overcoming doubts by overseas customers about the ability of a UK supplier to meet quality standards.

Quality assurance protagonists (including assessors such as BSI QA) generally do not endorse marketing benefits of ISO 9000 as a *reason* for seeking registration. This is on the grounds that any such gains may be too short-term to alone provide the necessary motivation to keep up the quality system. Moreover, it is argued that by an exclusive or main focus on the marketing aspects other important potential benefits may be missed. In their own decision to seek ISO 9000, P&O European Ferries, for example, recognised that any marketing advantages would be short-term and would not alone provide sufficient reasons for the effort involved in a formal quality system. Similarly, whilst Datac Adhesives use ISO 9000 as an effective marketing tool – the salesforce all carry a copy of the certificate – they sought and gained benefits on a much broader front.

We believe that ISO 9000 can be an effective marketing tool and there is no reason why any company should not use registration in this way. The Standard is a serious commitment to quality and in all markets quality is a very important issue. However, the fundamental marketing potential of ISO 9000 goes beyond just having and keeping the 'gong'. Marketing should be about far more than manipulating perceptions. The real marketing case for ISO 9000 is that companies will succeed because they really do take quality seriously. Implemented in the right way, a quality system to ISO 9000 makes for a quality company. Whilst as explained in Chapter 2, ISO 9000 is not itself a product or service standard, it does provide a framework for quality work and in the longer run for quality improvement.

EFFICIENCY THROUGH ISO 9000

The real marketing advantage of ISO 9000, therefore, may be that improvements in the operation of a business from an effective quality system will bring in profitable business – the objective of all marketing. This links into efficiency – ISO 9000 helps improve a company's overall efficiency and makes it 'fit for the race', a metaphor suggesting the need to be able to compete and stay in increasingly fast-moving markets.

The claim that ISO 9000 improves efficiency is rooted in 'getting it right – and getting it right first time'. As discussed in

Chapter 2, the important requirement of process control within the Standard implies that for any operation there is a best way of working and that once this is found, a system that ensures that this way is followed, improves efficiency and reduces waste. To do it wrong is to produce not quality products but rejects that must be scrapped or expensively reworked. John Axon at Park Farm, for example, believes that by defining the optimum feed regime for his cattle – and writing it down – he has significantly reduced the waste of food previously given to animals in excess of their true needs.

Some, however, may object that to believe that a 'best way' can be defined and defined for all or a long time, is to build in long-term inefficiency, since changing circumstances (including improved knowledge and technology) demand changes in methods of work. This of course is true and in any quality system 'best ways' have to be regarded as provisional until something better is proven. In the meantime, however, the defined way is followed. An effective quality system is not static, therefore, but builds in this necessary commitment to improvement. It is also though an anchor to keep the operation running until the changes are made.

Another aspect of defining effective process methods is consistency. If effective methods are defined they should be followed wherever appropriate – by all staff, on all shifts and across all sites. In this way variability is reduced. This is another way of saying that rejects are reduced, since rejects are, by definition, products with a variance exceeding defined limits. Kent County Council Highways and Transportation, for example, found a key benefit of ISO 9000 was consistency across projects, DHL International adopted and benefited from common methods in all depots and P&O European Ferries used their quality system to achieve a uniformity of approach in both UK and Continental ports.

A uniform approach and adherence to the best way is possible without a fully documented quality system – at least in a small organisation. However, even where very few are involved in an operation, written procedures are often more effective than faulty memory – John and Diane Axon at Park Farm have found it far better to have the feed mixes written down at the point where they are prepared. Any need for effective documentation will obviously increase as organisations grow in size, until at some point they become essential – the only way to have a common approach is to have one 'hymn sheet'. In larger operations, all those involved in an operation may never even meet let alone communicate – they may be on different sites or shifts.[1] In these circumstances consistency demands effective and correct documentation.

Of course, in the real world, problems will still occur even though an effective quality system is in place. No system is perfect and unanticipated situations will arise which the system was not designed to cover. Also, we live in a changing world and what is effective now may be less so tomorrow. The quality system approach recognises this to be the case and builds in mechanisms[2] to trace problems back to their source, find solutions and make effective changes. The solution may be concerned with rectifying the immediate problem – Datac Adhesive have used their quality system to relate batch problems to particular suppliers of raw materials. More importantly, the quality system mechanisms should investigate whether changes in methods are likely to reduce the chance of problems recurring. Organisations implementing an effective quality system change their approach to problems; from purely 'fire fighting' – getting over the latest crisis – to using problems as a spur to long-term improvement and efficiency. Kent County Council Highways and Transportation, for example, have recognised how such benefits have come from their commitment to investigate problems and by using the mechanisms provided by their quality system.

---

[1] The authors know of a site where problems of consistency in output from a plant were shown to be due to the day and evening shifts setting the plant to what they both believed to be correct. However, lacking written records of the settings, each shift had their own 'best' way.

[2] In particular the *quality triangle* approach described later (see Chapter 7).

Customer complaints are problems with in-built incentives to find remedies. Anyone wanting to stay in business must recognise that customers have to be kept at least minimally happy; complaints lead to lost business. Again, a quality system should lift a company's sights to finding long-term changes which reduce the problems leading to these customer complaints and, therefore, help improve efficiency. Of course, immediate solutions to make the customer happy (or less unhappy) are still essential but the philosophy is also to regard the complaint as an indicator of fundamental problems which need to and can be addressed.

An intrinsic aspect of improving efficiency is reducing costs. Efficiency gains either lead to a more cost effective way of doing the work in the first place or reduce waste. Waste has an obvious cost in lost raw materials and this is widely recognised. However, less often acknowledged is that waste is also a loss of labour time, plant utilisation and management effort; all used in producing the waste. In other words there is not only a direct cost but also an opportunity cost of rejects. For this reason, improvements in working methods, apart from any obvious reduced rejection rates, are another aspect of controlling inefficiency. The gain is real even though it may be difficult to measure (eg because systems are not in place for costing staff time).

A final comment on efficiency is that any gains in this area result from an effective quality system rather than registration to ISO 9000 as such. The Standard provides a model for a quality system which if implemented properly should produce efficiency (and some other) benefits whether or not it is independently assessed. A valid question in fact is why do organisations inflict assessment on themselves? Apart from any marketing gains from having ISO 9000 registration, the argument for assessment is largely to prove to the organisation that the quality system is working effectively. Also, perhaps it gives an additional incentive for adhering to the system; assessment and surveillance make sure the system is followed all the time and not just when it is easy to do so.

THE MANAGEMENT OF CHANGE

A key management task is adapting successfully to change. Change is essential to respond to forces outside and within an organisation and increasingly any business must be flexible and responsive to stay in the market. However, part of the task of managing change is ensuring that structures are in place so that change is positively directed and is not so badly coordinated that the organisation either flies apart or is paralysed. A quality system can provide a structure around which innovation can be successfully introduced and often it is the *implementation* of change rather than thinking of new ideas that is the problem. However, a quality system can also provide mechanisms for identifying the need for change – through monitoring problems of all sorts – and identifying effective responses.

The need for a quality system may be also recognised as a result of change. In their early days, businesses are often managed in every detail by their proprietors who effectively take all decisions of any importance. Quality standards may be very high because of this total personal involvement and commitment. Such businesses are likely to grow just because of this reputation but such success brings problems of its own. Sooner or later the owner of the business simply cannot take all decisions or be involved in all quality issues. He no longer has the capacity for this level of control. Often this precipitates a crisis – the owner blames his staff – 'the only way to get everything done is to do it yourself' – but is forced to rely on them. In turn the staff feel that they have no room to be responsible and committed because nothing is left to their own initiative. Many businesses fail to pass through this problem and either remain in some sort of no-growth state or fail altogether. Those that succeed are likely to replace spur of the moment control with an effective system which both controls and empowers staff to take responsibility.

These systems can take various forms but a quality system to ISO 9000 is a proven approach – the Standard provides an effective means of controlling growth but without impeding the capacity for effective change. Once installed the system can not only bring order into a crisis but can provide a framework for further growth and a continual response to a changing environment. P&O European Ferries (not of course a small business) regard this capacity to manage change as a key benefit of ISO 9000 – their business cannot stand still and the quality system has proved to be an effective vehicle for change.

As well as through organic growth, businesses expand by acquisition. Other businesses are brought in and have to be integrated. A quality system can provide a framework for this; much as it provides a common approach for different sites within an organisation. However, it should be remembered that an important feature of a quality system is that whilst it may meet the requirements of ISO 9000, above all else it must be designed to meet the unique needs of a particular organisation. An attempt to mechanically impose it upon an acquisition may, therefore, lead to more problems than it solves. Extension of a system in this way needs very careful planning.

As with the benefits of efficiency, using a quality system as means of managing change is independent of the issue of registration and assessment. At most, the relevance of independent assessment lies in providing an additional incentive to full and effective implementation.

HUMAN ISSUES

ISO 9000 has a reputation for being soulless and not people friendly. Staff may work to a quality system with a good grace or otherwise but it is not usually seen as a motivator. However, if well thought out, a quality system and ISO 9000 can be effective in the vital human resource side of a business.

One important benefit that is often missed is that the *process* of gaining ISO 9000 can have a strongly positive effect. P&O European Ferries, for example, found this aspect of the project to be a real gain – staff throughout the company were deeply involved in designing an effective system and shared the sense of achievement in gaining the Standard. As we shall strongly urge later in this book, successful design and implementation of a quality system must closely involve staff. This shared activity is an integrating force and may be the first time ever that staff at all levels have been involved in a strategic project. This not only produces effective solutions but is itself a powerful motivator. Staff opinion is taken seriously. Such benefits may be once-off and short-term but in practice staff involvement often becomes a habit. The commitment to solving problems and the specific mechanisms provided in a quality system will also encourage long-term participation.

Another aspect of ISO 9000 is that both designing and implementing a quality system will encourage staff to think about quality and quality issues. Commitment is essential to quality but the system can itself stimulate this. Even reviewing how each job is done at present (as we shall discuss later, an essential starting point for developing procedures) is likely to suggest the need for improvements. Moreover, the quality system becomes a reason for keeping to standards rather than bowing to mere management whim. Without a system, effective methods may be used, but they are often imposed from above and need far more policing than a system introduced with staff involvement. Defects of a quality system, on the other hand, should be recognised as a shared responsibility rather than someone else's problem.

A final human side of a quality system to ISO 9000 is that it can provide a framework for new staff (and, therefore, another aspect of managing change). An established team may well know the best way of working without referring to written procedures, but what happens when a new member joins? At best there will be quite a learning period during which mishaps are more likely. A written quality system helps by defining the tasks and the effective methods of carrying them out and in this sense is a valuable training resource.[3]

---

[3] As argued later, however, a procedure manual is not meant to be a training manual – it is for use by trained staff.

THE DISADVANTAGES

What are the disadvantages of an ISO 9000 approach to quality management? These clearly need thinking about before deciding whether or not to implement this type of system.

The most common criticism of ISO 9000 is that it is bureaucratic. Firms which have been pressured into achieving the Standard are reported to find it largely to be a matter of form filling and form filling for its own sake; quite irrelevant to real quality issues. A burden, it is said, on firms which were already well managed. That there is *some* truth in this charge cannot be denied. The Standard does specifically require written records relating to quality issues although these do not have to be forms – John Axon of Park Farm for example uses a wipe board to record some of his key data – it allows complete flexibility in the method of record keeping. Moreover, what records are kept is very largely a matter for each company to decide and even the smallest business finds that some relating to quality issues are required to meet the needs of the business, the requirements of customers or to comply with the law. At least an effective system will ensure that any records are well and consistently kept; there is no point at all in having incomplete and out of date data.

The charge of bureaucracy, therefore, is often very largely the consequence of a poorly designed system; it is needlessly bureaucratic because unnecessary form filling has been built into it or the particular form of record keeping is onerous because it is not well thought out. Often these sort of problems arose because management commitment and staff involvement was insufficient; perhaps the design of the system was largely left to a consultant. As we shall discuss later, consultants have a useful role in implementing a quality system, but they cannot take responsibility for its contents.

ISO 9000 is also said to be inflexible; either a quality system to the Standard is too inflexible to meet the needs of a particular business or that by having the system a business becomes inflexible and is not responsive to the demands of its market. Again, like the problem of bureaucracy, any such problem is nearly always a matter of poor design. The system is inflexible because the operational needs were not adequately thought through or the requirements of the Standard were misunderstood. For example, a requirement for a client to place an order in writing was perhaps built into the system. This may be a good practice but not if verbal orders are the way business is done in the industry – there is certainly nothing in the Standard requiring this type of inflexibility.

The charge of inflexibility also has another meaning – that everyone is expected to follow the system all the time. But this is a fundamental principle of a quality system and if a method is only sometimes appropriate it should either not form part of the system or the limits of its application should be defined.

That everyone is required to follow an ISO 9000 system is also often felt to be a very real problem for particular staff. Managers may well believe that a system approach is excellent for their staff to follow but not themselves – they do not feel the need to follow defined methods.

Highly skilled and creative staff often have the same problem. For a system to work, however, everyone must be committed to it and willing to comply with it. If this proves to be restrictive to managers and other staff in carrying out their work – they are 'form filling' rather than doing whatever they are paid to do – then the system should be changed. However, until the system is changed all staff covered by it must comply – if you don't like the system change it but until then follow it.

Such problems in following a system are likely to be most acute for managers or owners of small businesses where all significant issues, whether quality related or otherwise, were previously decided by the 'boss'. With a system in place he or she is transformed from a despot (benevolent or otherwise) into a constitutional ruler. This is generally beneficial all round but not an easy transition to make. Also the manager or owner (and this applies to collective board management as well) must be really committed to the system at both the design and implementation stages. It cannot just be left to a second tier with the senior

43

management left free of the details. The result of this is an ineffective system because management requirements are not built in. In other words a key group of the staff and their needs were not considered. Also, the management's lack of commitment will be signalled to the staff – if the boss doesn't believe in it (or follow it) why should we? And pretence will not work for long; especially in a small firm.

Often, the hands-off approach of management to a quality system is the result of lack of time rather than willingness. With the pressure of day-to-day business, there are insufficient hours in the day for the management to be involved in designing a system and later ensuring it is working effectively. Day-to-day business clearly must not be neglected – there is no point in having a well designed system but no work to put through it. The answer to this problem is not easy to give in general terms; improved time management skills may be part of the solution but it does sound too facile. All that can be said is that quality management is a core task of senior management and the long-term success of the organisation depends on getting it right. The governor of a city was once asked whether he intended to improve the drainage system. He replied that it was certainly his intention to do so eventually, but for the moment he was working night and day to deal with a cholera outbreak and could not spare the time. In all organisations time has to be somehow found for fundamental issues.

The final disadvantage of ISO 9000 to discuss is its cost. Not only, it is said, is this approach needlessly bureaucratic and inflexible but it is an unnecessary expense which companies are forced to pay to meet customer and other pressures. Certainly the process does have costs both explicit and implicit.

The explicit costs of ISO 9000 include payments to the assessment body and these are on-going rather than one off. In a later chapter these will be discussed in further detail. The charges made vary with the size and complexity of the firm assessed but for a firm with 50 or so employees the annual fee is likely to be around £2000 (1994 prices) and even for a very small business is likely to approach £1000. Another explicit cost is consultancy to guide the design and implementation of a system. Although not always essential, such bought-in advice is often felt to be required for one reason or another. This too is more likely to cost in terms of thousands rather than hundreds of pounds (although unlike assessment is largely a one off charge). There are also other more minor explicit costs such as training for the system and possibly various resources needed to implement it.

Explicit charges, however, are usually much less than the implicit costs of the staff time required to set up and run the system. Often these are unmeasured because the accounting mechanisms are not in place. These are another form of opportunity costs – the cost of time which might otherwise be spent in activities such as bringing in business. However, in practice, this opportunity cost may be quite low because the time on ISO 9000 is somehow squeezed in and would not otherwise be profitably spent (spent in the business that is). Also, with a well designed system, the staff time required to run the system should be kept to a minimum – for the large majority, following the system should be no more than doing their regular job.

The financial aspect of ISO 9000 is, moreover, not all a matter of costs. Hopefully there are some real monetary gains as well through efficiency improvements and extra business. These too, though, may be hard to quantify. Extra business may well result; perhaps from keeping business that is at risk if the Standard is not achieved or, more commonly, gaining new business – eg through 'opening doors'. Several of the businesses used as case studies in this book increased their turnovers following ISO 9000. However, it is difficult in these and other firms to definitely prove that the growth in sales is as a direct result of achieving the Standard. It may be coincidental or it may be an indirect consequence such as improved staff morale through participation in implementing the system. The efficiency savings may equally be difficult to measure. In a true manufacturing business any decline in scrap rates should be measurable at least in terms of wasted materials, although opportunity cost savings may be more difficult to quantify. These gains are even harder to quantify in service businesses.

Before commitment to ISO 9000, a company should attempt to draw up its own balance sheet of costs and benefits and make the best estimate possible of the figures likely to be involved. The more intangible benefits and any anticipated disadvantages also need carefully weighing. Only then can an informed decision be made.

4

The Requirements of ISO 9000

This chapter looks in some more detail at ISO 9000 and introduces the requirements of this Standard. These requirements and their practical application in a business are also the subject of Chapters 5, 6 and 7.

THE ISO 9000 SERIES OF PUBLICATIONS

So far we have referred to ISO 9000 as one Standard and by implication one document. In fact ISO 9000 is a series of publications, shown in Table 4.1.

The standards in the series are of two types; models – which are indicated in the table in italics – and guidelines. Assessment to the Standard is against one of the models and not the guidelines. Companies seeking ISO 9000 are required, therefore, to implement (and by implication have on file) the current version of the model they have selected to meet – ISO 9001 or 9002 or 9003. Familiarity with the other publications in the series is optional. For completeness we should also mention that there are other standards,[1] which are not part of the ISO 9000 series but which provide guidelines to aspects of implementing a quality system.

All these standards are approved and periodically revised and updated by official bodies after lengthy periods of consultation

---

[1] See ISO 10011–1/2/3 for quality system auditing, ISO 10012–1 for measuring equipment and ISO 10013 for quality manuals.

Table 4.1   The ISO 9000 series of Standards

ISO Reference	Subject
9000 – 1	Guidelines for selection and use of ISO 9000
9000 – 2	Guidelines for application of ISO 9000
9000 – 3	Guidelines for application of ISO 9001 to the development, supply and maintenance of software
9000 – 4	Dependability management
9001	*Model for quality assurance in design, development, production, installation and servicing*
9002	*Model for quality assurance in production, installation and servicing*
9003	*Model for quality assurance in final inspection and testing*
9004 – 1	Guidelines for quality system elements
Guidelines for:	
9004 – 2	Services
9004 – 3	Processed materials
9004 – 4	Quality improvements
9004 – 5	Quality plans
9004 – 6	Project management
9004 – 7	Configuration management

with a wide range of interested parties. As British Standards (eg BS EN ISO 9001 – formerly BS 5750 Part 1) they are approved and published by the British Standards Institution and as international standards by the International Organisation for Standardisation (ISO); a worldwide federation of national standard bodies. The only difference between the British and international versions is in the title and even this, in the 1994 version, follows the ISO practice – renamed from BS 5750 Part 1 to BS EN ISO 9001[2] etc. Most other developed countries have a national equivalent to ISO 9000 (eg DIN ISO 9000 in Germany). As mentioned in the introduction, throughout the book, we refer to the series of standards as ISO 9000.

---

[2] The EN part of the title is a reference to the European standard for quality assurance – EN 29000 – again the contents are identical.

ISO 9000 MODELS

The ISO 9000 series, therefore, includes three models or specifications for quality assurance systems. These are the same as the pre-1994 'parts' of BS 5750 – ISO 9001 is the revised equivalent of BS 5750 Part 1, ISO 9002 of Part 2 and ISO 9003 of Part 3. Assessment to the Standard is against one of these models. They are not, as is sometimes falsely believed, a hierarchy of grades to progress through. A company assessed to ISO 9002 for example, would not normally regard this as a preliminary to seeking ISO 9001.

The difference between the models is in the requirements included. ISO 9001 has the most comprehensive requirements and these are set out under 20 headings. ISO 9002 has 19 requirement headings; all those of ISO 9001 except for design. ISO 9003 is rather more limited and covers just 12 of the requirements. Table 4.2 shows the requirement headings included in each model. The contents and implications of each heading are touched upon later in this chapter and covered in detail in Chapters 5, 6 and 7.

A company implementing ISO 9000 must decide, early in the project, which of the three models is appropriate. Two sorts of considerations apply; the activities carried out by the organisation and the requirements of customers.

The activities of the organisation particularly apply to whether or not ISO 9001 is appropriate – if design activities of any sort (and as we shall discuss in Chapter 5, 'design' can be very widely interpreted) are not carried out then 9002 (or possibly 9003) rather than 9001 is clearly the relevant model. Also, even if design activities are carried out, it is likely that they will not be included in the assessment – 9002 rather than 9001 will be sought – if they do not form part of the contract with the client (again discussed in Chapter 5).

As discussed previously, customer expectations and requirements are often an important factor in deciding whether or not to consider ISO 9000 and it may be that customer views should be considered in selection of the particular ISO 9000 model

Table 4.2   Requirements of ISO 9000 models

Reference	Requirement	Model 9001	9002	9003
4.1	Management responsibility	*	*	*
4.2	Quality system	*	*	*
4.3	Contract review	*	*	
4.4	Design control	*		
4.5	Document and data control	*	*	*
4.6	Purchasing	*	*	
4.7	Control of customer supplied product	*	*	
4.8	Product identification and traceability	*	*	*
4.9	Process control	*	*	
4.10	Inspection and testing	*	*	*
4.11	Control of inspection, measuring and test equipment	*	*	*
4.12	Inspection and test status	*	*	*
4.13	Control of nonconforming product	*	*	*
4.14	Corrective and preventive action	*	*	
4.15	Handling, storage, packaging, preservation and delivery	*	*	*
4.16	Control of quality records	*	*	*
4.17	Internal quality audits	*	*	
4.18	Training	*	*	*
4.19	Servicing	*	*	
4.20	Statistical techniques	*	*	*

(although if there is no significant design work carried out 9001 rather than 9002 cannot be sensibly required). Such discussions with customers may help in the decision but take care that the real requirements are understood – it costs nothing for customers to prefer the more demanding 9001 model whether or not they have a true design need to be met. An alternative method of gauging market demand for one or other of the models may be to check the choice of other suppliers. For any industry or activity there is often a consensus on the appropriate ISO 9000 model.

The choice of model is an important decision and hopefully the explanations of the requirements for each, provided in this book, will be helpful. For convenience we shall generally discuss ISO 9000 in terms of the 9001 model. The 9002 model is identical except for the exclusion of the design element and all 12 requirements of the 9003 model are also included in 9001. Also selection of 9003 (rather than 9001 or 9002) is not common – its concentration on the testing aspects is not really a model for a full quality assurance system, which requires more than a focus on defects.

APPLYING AN ISO 9000 MODEL

Whichever model is selected, it must be applied so that it both meets the real needs of the organisation as well as the requirements of the Standard. One important issue, which has to be decided early on in designing a system, is its scope in relation to the boundaries and activities of the organisation. Another important set of decisions involve relating and interpreting the requirement headings of the Standard to the management structure and existing business of a company.

For most smaller companies there is little debate or uncertainty about the scope of the quality system in relation to organisation's boundary; ISO 9000 is applied to the whole of the company. Quite likely in a small company, all activities are based on a single site and departmental structure is minimal. Benfell Communications, for example, is a dealership based at one address and it would be impractical (even if desirable) to attempt to apply a quality system to an artificially separated part of the company. However, in larger companies, which are already structured in branches and divisions, it is quite possible to consider seeking ISO 9000 for only one part of the business. Kent County Council for example, has registered the Highways and Transportation Department to the Standard. DHL International on the other hand, could have chosen to register only one or a few branches but decided to include the whole company and all sites at one go. Where such decisions are realistic, limiting the scope of the system and registration in this way is an option which an organisation is quite free to exercise. A roll-out approach of initial implementation in selected units may also be used as a route to eventual organisation-wide coverage. One limitation of such an approach, however, is that the Standard can only be claimed – eg in advertising – for the units covered in the scope of the registration and not the whole company. In other words you cannot register your postroom and then claim or imply that the whole company has achieved ISO 9000 (it has been tried). The independent assessors who effectively award ISO 9000 will monitor a registered firm to ensure that there is no false claiming of this sort and they may also need to be convinced that the boundaries of selected units can be practically defined.

ISO 9000 can also be applied to part rather than all of the business activities (eg the product ranges) of a company – this is in effect only the same as applying it to an organisational division and the limitations just discussed equally apply – perhaps more so. However, another aspect of the scope of the Standard relates to the *functional* activities included in the quality system. Quality assurance and ISO 9000 focuses on activities directly relating to quality issues relevant to producing the product or service – agreeing the contract with a customer, design work, the production process itself, delivery and after sales are all examples of these sorts of activities. Businesses, however, are necessarily involved in other tasks as well. These include financial and accounting work, personnel, general administration and much of sales and marketing – having contracts to review usually involves much prior effort to gain the order. All these activities are essential to the survival and growth of the business but are not directly related to the quality of the final product or service and they are not included in the requirements of ISO 9000. However, procedures and rules can be applied in these areas as well and it may be decided that incorporation of some of these areas into the quality system is effective and efficient. Such a choice is a matter for each company and some may decide that a broader rather than narrower quality system is required. However, including such additional activities within the system may make implementation that much harder because of the wider span of procedures and the increased range of staff affected. Also, there may be implications for the assessment, although assessors may well not examine parts of a quality system which are not specifically a requirement of the Standard.

How each requirement of the Standard can be interpreted and applied to a business is the subject of the next three chapters. There is some logic to the sequence of the 20 headings under which these requirements are set out in the Standard. However, we consider it useful to rearrange the requirements of ISO 9001 into the three broad groupings shown in Figure 4.1 and it is on this basis that the discussion of the requirements is set out in Chapters 5, 6 and 7.

In the central block of the figure are listed the nine requirements which relate to the *operating process* of the organisation; what the company does, day to day, for its customers – eg sell and service mobile communications, manufacture adhesives, operate vehicle ferries, build and repair highways or raise cattle. In sequence, the activities of the operating process include some sales and marketing tasks, design (relevant to ISO 9001 rather than 9002), production, distribution and after sales. For each of these activities one or more of the Standard's requirements are relevant.

The right hand block of the figure shows the six requirements relating to *support activities* that are carried out to enable the operating process to function effectively. These are subdivided into quality resources and quality records.

Finally there are five requirements within the left hand *quality system control* box. When we come to consider the other 15 requirements in detail, it is very likely that most readers will recognise that to some extent, these are already met in their own organisation, even if documented procedures have never been prepared. Also, most of the requirements should seem as no

53

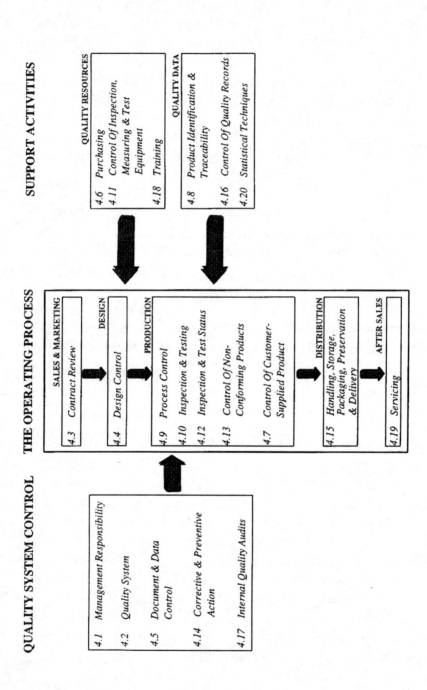

QUALITY SYSTEM CONTROL   **THE OPERATING PROCESS**   **SUPPORT ACTIVITIES**

QUALITY RESOURCES

4.6   Purchasing
4.11 Control Of Inspection, Measuring & Test Equipment
4.18 Training

QUALITY DATA

4.8   Product Identification & Traceability
4.16 Control Of Quality Records
4.20 Statistical Techniques

SALES & MARKETING

4.3   Contract Review

DESIGN

4.4   Design Control

PRODUCTION

4.9   Process Control
4.10 Inspection & Testing
4.12 Inspection & Test Status
4.13 Control Of Non-Conforming Products
4.7   Control Of Customer-Supplied Product

DISTRIBUTION

4.15 Handling, Storage, Packaging, Preservation & Delivery

AFTER SALES

4.19 Servicing

4.1   Management Responsibility
4.2   Quality System
4.5   Document & Data Control
4.14 Corrective & Preventive Action
4.17 Internal Quality Audits

Figure 4.1   Requirements of ISO 9001

more than good common business sense. The quality system control requirements are, however, rather different because they only make sense in the context of a formal and documented quality system.

AIDS TO INTERPRETING ISO 9000

Anyone planning a quality system needs to understand how the Standard should be applied in their particular type of business activity. The ISO 9000 series, as already mentioned, does provide some guidance of this sort. Anyone considering ISO 9001 for a software writing business, for example, should certainly consult ISO 9000–3 and a service business may find ISO 9004–2 helpful.[3] There are, however, some other sorts of guides and 'translation documents' which may be very useful or even essential reading.

One example is schemes for stockists. ISO 9002 (rather than 9001 since stockists generally have no design function) is quite commonly sought by various types of stockists – businesses which buy in and stock products for re-sale. High street retailers are of course stockists but are less likely to seek ISO 9000 than suppliers to other businesses such as builders' merchants and steel stockholders. In detail, such businesses vary widely but all have many features in common when implementing the Standard and especially in relation to purchasing, safeguarding stock and being able to trace product sources. The assessment for stockists is against the relevant model for quality assurance (ie 9002) but to help such businesses implement the standard, as well as assist in assessment work, several of the assessment bodies, including BSI QA, have prepared and published stockists' schemes. A stockist type business is likely to treat these documents as the standard to be followed even if strictly speaking this is not the case.

The various stockists' schemes have wide application across businesses dealing in all sorts of different products. Another sort

---

[3] There are also the general guidance standards in the ISO 9000 (eg ISO 9000–1) series which may be useful in planning a quality system for any business.

of interpretation document is much narrower and focuses on a very specific industry or type of business. There is for example a document to guide the application of ISO 9000 in solicitors' practices – *Quality: A Briefing For Solicitors*[4] and equivalents have been prepared in many other fields. These both translate the meaning of the requirements of the Standard and provide guidance on how these can be practically implemented in the particular type of business – eg what does design mean in a solicitor's work? Such documents are generally prepared by a trade association or professional body (eg the Law Society) and may well bear the approval of one or more assessment bodies. Where such approval is given, following the guidelines may avoid some of the problems of assessment which can otherwise arise – eg the meaning of a particular requirement within the context of an industry. However, it should be remembered that the assessment is against the Standard itself and not the translation document. Also, strictly speaking, any endorsement by one assessment body is valid for that body and not others – for example BSI QA approval of a particular interpretation does not commit SGS Yarsley or any of the other bodies. In practice, however, a document endorsed by one body is likely to be a reasonable guide for the industry concerned.

Anyone planning an ISO 9000 system should, at an early point in the project, find out if any of this type of translation and interpretation work has been carried out in their own industry.

---

[4] Published by the Law Society (1993).

5

Operating Process Requirements

As shown in Figure 5.1 there are nine requirements of ISO 9000 which relate to the operating process of an organisation – what a business does day to day for its customers.

In this chapter we discuss these nine requirements in turn. Each is titled as it is in the Standard and the number is the reference nomenclature. Our intention in discussing each requirement is to indicate only in broad terms what is covered and what, in practice, it means to apply the requirement in a business. Anyone planning a quality system must also read the relevant, published model (ie ISO 9001 or 9002) and is also advised to consult any available interpretation document for their own industry.

CONTRACT REVIEW (4.3)

Underlying quality and quality assurance is the importance of meeting customer requirements. Clearly a pre-requisite of this is ensuring that both the customer and all parts of the supplier organisation have a common understanding of the requirement. Also the supplier should be confident that the customer's requirement can be met. In essence, contract review concerns this part of the business process with specific reference to *reviewing* that requirements have been adequately defined, agreed and are within the capability of the business. There is also a reference covering amendments to the contract; any subsequent changes must also be agreed and those involved with the order must understand them. Finally, there is a reference to maintaining

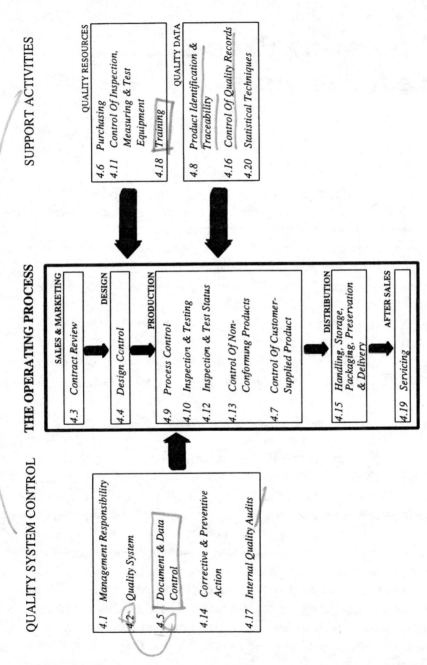

Figure 5.1 Operating process requirements of ISO 9001

records of the review and in practice this is often largely met as part of the contract documentation.

The requirement for contract review covers any form of contract. This does not have to be a long document or for that matter even a written order. In some businesses, contracts are lengthy and in writing (eg for major plant) but in others may take the form of short written quotations. Some businesses work well with purely verbal orders taken over the phone or in person. There is no requirement for a firm seeking ISO 9000 to change its basis of business and demand that customers start to place orders in writing or even to start sending out confirmation notes if this serves no useful pupose. However, there is a presumption that orders are recorded in some form but in most cases this is unlikely to require any real change – how can orders be processed if there is no record? This might take the form of works instructions or in the case of a business supplying from stock, details passed to dispatch. In a self service type of business where the customer selects the item himself even this might not be needed.

It should be noted that the requirement is concerned with contract *review* rather than preparing the contract itself and therefore it implies that each order is systematically considered to ensure that the details of the requirement are adequately defined and that the business is able to meet them. However, this does not have to mean that a new bureaucratic stage in the ordering process is required since any orders taken are presumably already read by someone before they are processed and those involved in this activity can often be considered to be carrying out the review.

For most businesses, meeting the requirements for contract review are unlikely to necessitate significant changes in established practice. Establishing what the customer wants and making sure the customer knows what you will supply is obviously good business practice. Often, any change will mean no more than such good practice becomes standard and the problems arising from any misunderstandings of this sort are largely eliminated. Ensuring that good practice becomes standard is a principle running through ISO 9000.

DESIGN CONTROL (4.4)

The inclusion of the requirement for design control is the only difference between ISO 9001, which includes design control and 9002, which does not. This requirement is, however, both extensive and demanding and in the initial stages of planning a quality system, careful thought needs to be given to whether there is a design activity at all and whether it should be included within the assessment. Of all the UK firms registered to ISO 9000, the large majority have 9002 rather than 9001 (ie the old BS 5750 Part 2 rather than Part 1) and, therefore, do not include any design activities.

The underlying concept of design in the Standard is (as is much else) based on engineering practice with a distinct department developing design solutions to meet a customer's need, documenting this in a formal way, possibly producing prototypes and through this stage or otherwise, empirically testing the final product before it goes into production. However, the general principles of design can be applied in almost all businesses including services. A management consultancy for example plans a programme to meet the objectives of the work being carried out for a client and solicitors plan a case to achieve the best outcome for their client (in the guide to the Standard prepared by the Law Society, the term 'case planning' is used rather than design). In both these examples there is no design department as such but throughout work for clients, general principles are applied to meet unique needs. In these and other cases a feature of the 'design' work is that the requirement for it is an intrinsic part of the service for a particular client. In other words it is part of the contract with the client; design or case planning is carried out to meet the needs of a specific and identified client or customer.

Whether there is a need for design work of any sort as an implicit or explicit requirement of the contract is an important consideration in deciding whether ISO 9001 rather than 9002 is appropriate. Many businesses have a design function which develops new standard products, offered to customers in general. Car manufacturers produce a range of models and customers select one that best meets their individual needs. In this case, the customer requirement is expressed in terms of a concrete product and the work of the design team is not related to the needs of any particular customer. In contrast, where design work is undertaken for a specific customer or client the need is likely to be expressed in terms of performance criteria – a need for plant to carry out certain processes, a solution to a business problem or a favourable result in a legal case. The design control requirement of ISO 9001 is primarily concerned with work carried out to meet the needs of a specific customer and where carrying out design work is part of the contract.[1] In deciding between ISO 9001 or 9002 (ie whether or not to include design activities), therefore, it is not just a matter of whether or not design work is carried out but whether it forms part of the requirements of individual customers. Where design work is concerned only with producing a standard range of products, ISO 9002 rather than 9001 is usually more appropriate and the design activities need not be covered in the scope of the ISO 9000 assessment. ISO 9002 rather than 9001 also of course applies where no sort of design work is carried out – eg where the customer provides the design; the case in much sub-contracting work.

The requirement for design control is set out in the Standard under eight sub-headings each relating to an aspect of design work. *Design and development planning (4.4.2)* and *organisational and technical interfaces (4.4.3)* are concerned with ensuring the design team is adequately resourced and that it communicates with other groups in the organisation (interfaces). These requirements include a need for formal plans to ensure this is achieved. However, this does not mean that the whole process has to be fundamentally rethought for each design project; often standard plans and procedures can be applied to most or all of the work.

The *design input (4.4.4)* is the specification for the design work and this may have been established in some detail at the contract

---

[1] In some businesses such as consulting engineers, architects and design practices, the design work constitutes a high proportion or even all the work carried out for the client.

61

review stage. Since we are concerned with design carried out as part of the contract, it certainly will have already been considered to some extent at that stage, but further discussions with the customer may be needed, possibly to ensure the detailed requirement is sufficiently understood. There is also a requirement at this stage to take account of any statutory or regulatory requirements which affect the design or final product. What these might be will obviously vary widely from business to business and may not be specifically referred to by the customer (arguably they are an implicit customer requirement) but there is an onus on the supplier to identify such requirements. As well as the law, sources may include generally recognised codes of practice applying in a particular field.

Design output (4.4.5) covers how the design is expressed and documented. Specific reference is made to the need for the output to relate to the input (the requirement), to include a methodology for establishing that the design is effective (acceptance criteria), to explicitly identify aspects of the design relating to the safe operation of the final product and to include a review of the design documentation before it is passed on to other parts of the operation (to ensure that its form is appropriate). The actual form of design outputs can vary very widely between different types of business and may include drawings, technical descriptions, production specifications and computer files. However, an important implication is a need to ensure that it is the latest design version which is passed on to production and that revised designs replace earlier versions; a specific clause – *design changes (4.4.9)* – covers this.

The remaining requirements of design control all relate to various forms of checking which must be built into the whole process. *Design review (4.4.6)* is required to ensure that the design work and output *does* meet the design input; that requirements have been met. This activity often takes the form of a meeting of those principally involved in the design work and this has to be documented in some form so that there is evidence that a review has been carried out. The minimum requirement here is a review at the end of the process but it can also be carried out at stages throughout the work. *Design verification (4.4.7)* focuses on specific elements of the design and establishes if they will work as intended – is it effective bearing in mind what is required? This verification may involve testing the design through alternative and independent calculations, comparisons with similar and proven designs and carrying out various tests. In the case of some professional services 'objective' tests of designs may not be possible (eg a training company's course programme) and verification may be more a matter of judgement – perhaps checking by a colleague or more senior member of staff or in the case of the course programme, a dry run in-house. The results of verification may be formally considered at review meetings.

Finally, *design validation (4.4.8)* takes testing to the final stage and focuses on the final product made to the design. It is concerned to ensure that this meets customer requirements – design may be an intrinsic part of contract but usually it is the final product which really interests the customer – does it work and does it match the need? The requirement includes a need to test the design under defined operating conditions; it is not enough that the product works in some circumstances, it must work in the conditions under which the customer intends to use it. A boat may be fine in sheltered waters but inadequate for crossing the Atlantic. Where the design leads to a number of units being made, validation will often involve prototype testing with modifications made as required. Validation, however, becomes more difficult where the final product is a one off although commissioning tests and subsequent modifications may meet the need. Also, in such cases, the results of a particular project can be used as data in the verification if not validation of subsequent projects. Kent County Council Highways and Transportation, for example, has a system of feedback from each project to provide continuous improvement in its design work. In professional services and similar businesses, validation may be especially problematical since the final service cannot in practice be meaningfully tested under operating conditions before final use; a solicitor cannot request a dummy run of a court trial to test the validity of the defence case. The training course company may treat customer feedback from running the course as a form of validation but unless the course is to be re-run, the results are too late to enable that design to be changed. Businesses of this type are advised to follow any specific guidance produced for their industry or discuss the matter with their assessors.

It should now be apparent why the design requirements of ISO 9001 are considered to be demanding and why any business is advised to be certain that it is ISO 9001 rather than 9002 that is appropriate. However, design control, in practice, need not be daunting and in many businesses, analysis of existing methods is likely to show that the requirements are largely met and that the only major change lies in documenting the procedures followed and perhaps improving the methods of recording inputs, outputs and the results of already adequate testing.

PROCESS CONTROL (4.9)

Process control lies at the heart of the quality assurance concept and involves defining how activities with an implication for the quality of the product or service should be carried out. It involves developing effective procedures to control the operation. All parts of the total process are covered by this requirement except those specifically covered by other requirements (especially design but also handling, storage, etc and servicing). An important objective in implementing this requirement is to achieve a consistent quality in the product. John Axon of Park Farm, for example, recognises the importance of defining optimum feeding for his cattle and having procedures in place to ensure these are followed consistently rather than relying on memory and guesswork.

The specifics of this requirement include the need to define suitable processes, make sure the resources and equipment needed are available, and establish methods of monitoring to ensure the processes are carried out in the right way. In some types of jobbing businesses the appropriate processes to produce the product may need planning in each case and as well as the need for planning, the Standard refers to a need for a system of approval; eg the choice has to be confirmed by a suitably qualified person. However, in other types of businesses the process followed may be standard for each order and general procedures can be followed in each case without any significant extra planning or approval stage. Where the process involves physical equipment – machines etc – planning will involve the selection of appropriate equipment and making sure it is set up for the particular work. There is also a need to ensure that the equipment is adequately maintained and this is particularly important where variations in the operation of the equipment may affect the quality of output – eg tolerances.

Maintenance must be adequate to ensure the process can be carried out and this may entail a programme of preventative maintenance. However, in other cases adequate maintenance may be no more than procedures to ensure the equipment is fixed if and when it goes wrong; this would be entirely suitable for equipment that clearly either works or does not and where in the event of a failure of one machine others are available for the work. Where a physical product is not produced, eg in professional services, production equipment may not be involved at all and therefore some of these requirements cannot be practically met. However, increasingly, even businesses with an intangible final output now use computers in their work. These are in effect their process equipment.

Process control also involves monitoring the process to ensure that it is being followed in the right way. This may lead to a need for a record of readings taken whilst the process is being followed. In other cases, however, all that may be needed, in practice, is some method of establishing that the process has been followed. In this context the Standard refers to 'special processes'. These are defined as those where the results of the process cannot be fully established by testing the resulting product. This applies to some types of physical production but, often, especially to services – in professional services what is often important is that correct methodology has been followed and this may not be apparent in the final output. Where such special processes are present the requirement for process monitoring is given particular emphasis.

As in other requirements, process control refers to the need for documented procedures to define how work is to be carried out. These will often need to include or link to standards of workmanship which define what is appropriate for each piece of work – work instructions and samples may be appropriate.

INSPECTION AND TESTING (4.10)

Inspection and testing is very much bound up with process control, although in this case the emphasis is on the output of the process rather than how the process is carried out. In practice, most companies implementing a quality system are likely to develop procedures for each stage of their processes, which both define how the process is to be carried out (process control) and what tests are to be carried out on the output of each stage (inspection and testing). The form of inspecting and testing that is appropriate will clearly vary widely according to the nature of the business and the products concerned. In some, physical testing of the product (or samples) against objective technical parameters will be needed but in other cases (often in service businesses) simple inspection or checking will be adequate or all that is possible.

The nature of such inspection and testing must, therefore, be determined and incorporated into the procedures. Another general issue is the degree or overall level of inspection and testing. This must be sufficient to ensure that the customers' requirements are met but there are serious practical problems and costs of over-inspecting. In developing procedures it is easy to think of tests that *can* be carried out, but are they really essential to ensure that requirements are met? Similarly the requirement refers to the need for records to be kept of the inspection and testing work carried out, but again, in planning a system, there are dangers in insisting on too many and too detailed records. Kent County Council Highways and Transportation, for example, have recognised that their initial quality system included excessive levels of checking and too much associated paperwork.

The Standard refers to three areas where inspection and testing is required; receiving, in-process and final inspection and testing. Any business will buy in materials or other supplies which are incorporated into their own process; for example chemicals used in the production of adhesives, animal feedstuff or food used to prepare customers' meals. Clearly, the quality of the final output will be very much influenced by the quality of these inputs 'received' from outside. Inspection and testing may involve checking each delivery or samples. However, specific reference is also made in the Standard to the control exercised by the supplier of the input product and the implication is that the assurance of adequate controls (eg a formal quality system) may reduce the need to check incoming products from that supplier. *output*

In-process inspection and testing is that which is closely linked to process control, with the output of one process checked before it moves on to be an input into the next process.

Final inspection is of the complete product and service. This may include additional tests (eg that the various parts have been correctly assembled and that the final product works). However, any such final tests should normally be additional and not wastefully duplicate those carried out earlier. Final inspection and testing may also include ensuring that all in-process checks have been carried out with satisfactory results and this will involve a review of the test records. In the case of many services, no physical final inspection may be possible at all and instead someone with the appropriate authority signs off the project to signify that the quality procedures and plans have been followed. *CF role*

The concept of inspection and testing in the Standard implies that at each stage, any checks that apply in a particular case are normally carried out completely before the product moves on to the next stage of the process. However, a practical problem may arise in meeting a short timetable (which may also be part of the customer's requirement). Possibly the results of a test may take some time to analyse and in the meantime the production process cannot be delayed. This sort of problem can be associated with receiving, in-process or final inspection. The Standard acknowledges the possibility of these sort of problems and allows for products which are not fully tested to be processed, providing that procedures are devised to identify the products concerned so that they can be recalled if test results subsequently prove to be unsatisfactory.

INSPECTION AND TEST STATUS (4.12)

This requirement follows logically from the one just discussed. Having gone to all the trouble of having inspecting or testing procedures, it is clearly essential to know which tests have been carried out to date (with satisfactory results) on a product or service and to ensure that it normally only passes to the next stage of the process or to the customer after the appropriate checks have been carried out. The methods used can include markings on the product or entries on a job card or job file or segregated areas within the working area – Benfell Communications, for example, has signed areas for this purpose.

CONTROL OF NONCONFORMING PRODUCT (4.13)

Inspection and testing can be regarded as means of identifying products or services which do not match their specifications – nonconforming products. Two things need to done in such cases; make sure these products are identified as nonconforming and then decide what is to be done about them.

The purpose of clearly identifying nonconforming products or services is to make sure that they do not become mixed up with good product and passed off as such, either in subsequent stages of the process or, still worse, delivered to the customer. The methods of achieving this may include segregated or quarantine areas within the workshop, physically marking the product as nonconforming or entries on job cards or files; anything as long as it effectively prevents the work from being treated as if it is satisfactory.

A decision then needs to be made about what is to be done with nonconforming product. Options include scrapping, repairing or reworking to make them satisfactory (with the relevant inspection and tests repeated) or passing the faulty product to the customer but clearly identifying it as below standard and probably with adjustments in the charges made (concessions). Products might also be sold to different customers as seconds – some market traders specialise in this business (and hint whose 'quality' rejects are on their stall). These options for the treatment of nonconforming product also apply to a greater or lesser extent in services. In professional or knowledge services there may be a special need to safeguard confidential information in any documents which are scrapped. The Standard requires that such reviews of nonconforming product shall be carried out in a defined way (ie there shall be a procedure) including authority for making the decisions.

The idea of quality assurance also implies that the causes of nonconforming product should be considered to reduce future scrap rates or reworking. P&O European Ferries for example follows up faulty food materials (in their restaurants) by immediately faxing from the ship. However, this sort of follow-up from nonconforming product is really part of meeting another requirement – *corrective and preventive action* – discussed in Chapter 7.

CONTROL OF CUSTOMER-SUPPLIED PRODUCTS
(4.7)

The last requirement relating to production activities has only fairly specialised applications. In some businesses customers supply materials to a supplier and require them to be incorporated in the final product or service provided. Examples include components for including in larger assemblies (eg in the motor industry) or sending out products for finishing work such as shotblasting, plating, coating and dyeing. In professional services the customer-supplied product could be information – eg sales records given to a marketing consultant – which is in turn 'incorporated' along with other data collected from other sources. However, many businesses are not involved in such customer-supplied product and, therefore, all they need do in their quality system is to identify that this is the case.

The requirement for customer-supplied product has three strands. Firstly there is a need to ensure, through identification procedures, that the customer's material is incorporated in his product and nobody else's. If you supply a decorator with special paint, you will not be pleased if it is used in someone else's building. Secondly there is a need to make sure that the material does not deteriorate and is kept securely between being delivered and used in the production process. In the case of information supplied by a professional service client the concern may be one of confidentiality. Finally, there is an implied need to make sure the quality assurance procedures for any incoming material (ie receiving inspection) are also applied or adapted to cover customer supplied product. Otherwise, faults in this material could compromise the quality of the final product. For commercial reasons, dealing with nonconforming customer material may need a different approach than is used for faulty deliveries from outside suppliers.

HANDLING, STORAGE, PACKAGING, PRESERVATION AND DELIVERY (4.15)

Having produced the product or service and followed the quality system procedures applying to the various processes, it is important to ensure that there is no deterioration of the product before it is finally handed over to the customer – during what is often the distribution phase of the overall operation. Stages between the end of production and final delivery and where things might go wrong, include in storage (eg the stock of finished products), through poor packaging while it is in storage or in transit and in the delivery arrangements. Through these stages, the handling methods of the product need to be suitable and positive steps may have to be taken to ensure the product stays in good and useable condition. This requirement of the Standard covers all these areas, with a sub-clause for each (eg *handling – 4.15.2*), and relevent procedures are required.

The appropriate methods of handling, storing, packaging, preserving and delivering products obviously vary enormously between different types of business. What is suitable for quarry stone is quite unlike what is needed for electronic equipment or food. In nearly all cases the established methods of the industry or business will be adequate to meet the requirements of the Standard.

Many service businesses have quite limited involvement in these activities – often the service is not stored before delivery and there are no real handling problems. The packaging and delivery of documents produced as part of such a service may require no more than standard office practice. Preservation may be more a matter of ensuring confidentiality of information than preventing deterioration, although back-up copies of vital documents may be required. Although, therefore, this requirement of the Standard applies to such as professional services as much as any other business, meeting it may involve very little in the way of special procedures.

A final point is that this requirement refers to the handling, storage and preservation of the final product. There is also a comparable need to safeguard the product whilst it is in process as well as the materials used in its production. Appropriate methods and procedures are also needed at these stages but it is different requirements of the Standard which have to be met (eg *process control – 4.9*).

SERVICING (4.19)

The final stage of the operating process is servicing products after delivery to the customer – eg Benfell Communications'

maintenance of mobile phones. This is only a specified requirement in some types of businesses (in which case it will be
normally covered in the contract with the customer) and if
servicing is not provided there is obviously no need to start offering it just to meet the Standard (the quality system would,
instead, simply identify that this is the case and that the requirement, therefore, cannot be practically met). However, some
thought might be needed to ensure that there is no implied
service requirement. Management consultants, for example, do
not need to go out to clients to repair broken reports but they
may need to be able to respond to queries, arising from their
recommendations, some period after the end of the project.

Where any requirement for servicing exists, procedures have to
be established to cover the work involved, to provide records of
what is done for customers and to define appropriate verification
methods to ensure that any such requirements are met satisfactorily.

The sole or principal activity of some businesses is after sales
servicing (some manufacturers meet their servicing requirements
by sub-contracting to a specialist of this sort) and in such cases it
is the more comprehensive requirements relating to 'production'
(especially *process control – 4.9*) which would need to be met
rather than 'servicing' as such.

6

Support Activity Requirements

Chapter 5 considered the requirements of ISO 9000 in the operating process of a business. We now turn to the six requirements which concern support activities carried out to enable the operating process to work effectively. As shown in Figure 6.1 these include those relating to the provision of key resources and those concerned with the data arising from the operation of quality assurance.

PURCHASING (4.6)

Much of the content and value of any product is in the bought-in materials and components. A quality system must take account of the acquisition of these inputs which can so crucially affect the quality of the final product. It is no good carrying out your own process in a carefully controlled way if no care is taken of where the materials used come from. The purchasing function covers the process of acquiring these supplies. The work involved and the complexity of controlling it can be considerable. Datac Adhesives, for example, buys in over 500 materials from over 200 separate suppliers to provide the chemicals and other materials required in its processes.

To clear up potential misunderstandings in reading the Standard's requirements for purchasing, it should be noted that 'purchased product' – what purchasing procedures relate to – covers the widest meaning and includes all types of services as well as physical materials. This could include the services of free-

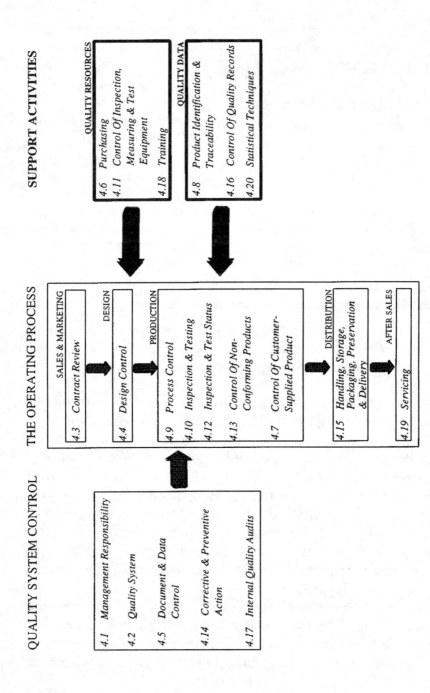

Figure 6.1 Support activity requirements of ISO 9001

lance workers although arguably they can equally be treated as employees[1] for the purposes of the quality system (but then they fall within the training requirement of the Standard discussed below). Products and services covered within the purchasing system, however, can be limited to those with a direct impact on the quality of the final product. Such supplies as stationery (but not where documents are the final output) and office cleaning might, for example, be regarded as falling outside the scope of the requirement. However, in practice, it may be simpler to apply the same purchasing procedures to all supplies.

Another potentially confusing term is 'sub-contractor'. This simply covers any type of supplier and is not restricted to the more specialist sense of the term. The reason 'supplier' is not used is that this term, in the Standard, covers the organisation implementing the quality system.

There are three sub-clauses covering the purchasing require-ment – *evaluation of sub-contractors (4.6.2), purchasing data (4.6.3)* and *verification of purchased product (4.6.4)*. Evaluation of sub-contractors is concerned with controlling suppliers – making sure that purchases are made from a source which is considered to be able to meet requirements and offer an adequate quality of pro-duct. This includes both selection of suitable suppliers and some form of continual assessment of their performance. As mentioned earlier in the book and contrary to some beliefs, there is no requirement to only buy from an ISO 9000 registered supplier. However, in evaluating the capability of a potential supplier, their methods of ensuring consistency of quality, including any quality assurance system in place, is certainly relevant and might well be a criterion for selection of at least a major supplier. The Standard acknowledges that the degree of rigour in selection and control is likely to vary depending on how critical the material supplied is in the quality of the final product. Also, the nature of the product supplied is relevant; in some cases the potential for quality varia-

---

[1]   The definition of freelance versus employed workers can be a matter of contention with the Inland Revenue and DSS. The inclusion of such suppliers within a formal purchasing system, including documented orders, *may* be regarded as *one* justification for their self-employed status.

tion may be quite low (eg office stationery for a service company) and the need to exercise tight control over the source may be rather less. Another point about the selection of suppliers is that the evidence of a long history of satisfactory service can often be considered very adequate and sufficient criteria for selection and this applies particularly when a quality system is being developed; there is no need to subject every supplier you have dealt with happily for years to a searching examination.

However they are selected, the generally used method to ensure that only these suppliers are used is the approved list. After initial vetting, selected suppliers are included on the list (someone has the defined authority to add to or remove from the list) and products can normally only be purchased from listed companies (the list of course being available to all involved in ordering). However, most businesses would find this method, by itself, to be too restrictive and there is often a procedure for buying unusual items from other suppliers approved by a special procedure (eg a senior manager's authority).

As well as methods for selection, there has to be a method of continually evaluating the performance of suppliers. This may take the form of a periodic review, with any documentary records arising from the deliveries considered (eg complaints made to the supplier) or an on-going system of assessing performance in each delivery made. Datac Adhesives, for example, operates a continuous scoring system for suppliers (with scores given based on defined performance criteria). This system includes a feedback of the cumulative score to the supplier and action taken (eg meetings with suppliers) when the score falls. Such feedback is not required by the Standard but is a very positive approach and better than simply stopping dealing with a supplier, without prior warning, when it is considered that performance has dropped below an acceptable level. However evaluation is carried out, there is a requirement to record the results. Without this it is difficult to imagine how it could ever be effective.

The requirements for purchasing data often amount to the placing of written orders including adequate details of what is required. In most cases this will be considered as no more than sensible business practice; it is far easier to dispute an unsatisfactory delivery if there is a written record of what was asked for in the first place. However, in businesses where orders are normally placed over the phone there is no need to change the practice (it may be the only effective way of buying) although some form of written record that the order has been placed is needed. Similarly, a product may be bought face-to-face 'as seen' and perhaps confirmed by no more than a handshake (eg cattle buying) and again there is no need to change an effective system by insisting on the exchange of a written order. Again, however, some form of record of the transaction will be required to meet the Standard.

Verification of purchased product applies in only certain purchasing situations; where it is agreed with the supplier that the product quality is to be checked by the purchaser *at the suppliers' premises*. Similarly it may be agreed with a customer (and covered in the contract) that he shall have the right to check at the premises of suppliers, materials or services which are to be included in the final product (eg a market research client checks the work of a specialist computer bureau to which this part of the process has been sub-contracted by the research agency). It should be stressed, however, that either form of verification applies only where this is agreed; either with the supplier or with the customer and in many businesses this will simply not be relevant. Finally, it should be made clear that this type of verification requirement is different to the receiving inspection discussed in Chapter 5 and as specified in *receiving inspection and testing (4.10.2)*. However, such checking of incoming materials obviously links into purchasing as a whole and often provides the data used in supplier evaluation (eg through details of nonconforming products).

CONTROL OF INSPECTION, MEASURING AND TEST EQUIPMENT (4.11)

At least where physical products are concerned, inspection and testing procedures (to meet *inspection and testing – 4.10* as discussed in Chapter 5) will almost always involve using equipment to take and record the measurements which establish whether product characteristics are within the required ranges. This covers a very wide range of equipment including such as micrometers, depth gauges and oscilloscopes. Computer software might also be used for test purposes although it should be noted that software used as an element in the process itself (eg word processing to produce legal documents) is outside the scope of this requirement. The use of inspection and testing equipment is less clear cut in the case of intangible services. Management consultants, for example, may well be able to claim that no such equipment is used in their business and, therefore, that this requirement cannot be applied. However, physical measurement may form part of an ancillary side of the service and in this case, the devices used may fall into the scope of this requirement – eg a market research company may keep test products in temperature controlled conditions and, therefore, need to consider calibrating thermometers. Also, some professional services (eg solicitors) have chosen to relate this requirement to methods of keeping staff up to date in their skills.

Wherever any type of inspection, testing or measuring equipment is used, there is a clear need to ensure that the readings taken are accurate or more strictly within the range of accuracy required by the process – in engineering, dimensions may need to be to several decimal places of a millimetre but in farming the nearest shovelful may be good enough. Generally, such checking of accuracy or calibration involves measuring against some standard (eg a known and standard metre length) and the requirement refers to the need, where possible, to trace back to an established and recognised national or international standard.

The scope of the control procedures set out in the Standard to meet this requirement are quite extensive and will often be found demanding – Datac Adhesives, for example, had to resolve some problems in this area at the time of their assessment. This will particularly be the case where there is an extensive and varied range of equipment involved. Specifically, procedures are required to cover:

○ Defining the nature and method of measurements to be taken as part of inspection and testing and setting tolerance levels.

○ The selection of suitable equipment for testing activities.

○ Defining methods and a programme of calibration for this equipment. Keeping records of this work and making sure it is done correctly.

○ Identifying all equipment in use and having a system for showing its calibration status (eg is it clear that this micro-meter has been calibrated within the specified period)?

○ Where equipment is found to be out of calibration, carrying out reviews to consider the consequences for the quality of product tested with the equipment – possibly it will not be adequate and customers may need informing of the problem.

Some of the work involved in calibration may be quite specialised and it may be necessary (or better) to use an independent specialist. Such suppliers may well be able to provide some of the information needed to develop and document effective procedures in this area. Guidance on methods may also be found in ISO 10012 – a standard for measuring equipment used in quality assurance.

TRAINING (4.18)

Staff are a major resource of all businesses and in the case of some services are the only significant one. Quality work demands that staff are skilled and capable of doing their job. Although most personnel matters are outside the scope of ISO 9000, there is a specific requirement for training. Training includes both skills required to carry out quality assurance tasks (eg inspection work) and those required to operate the processes covered by the quality system – operators being trained for the work they are employed to do. It also covers management and supervisory tasks.

The areas of training covered by the Standard are the identification of needs, carrying out any necessary training and keeping records. In the case of new staff, the training need (what is required so that they are capable of carrying out their new work) may be identified at the selection or induction interview but it is not satisfactory for that assessment to be the only one carried out whilst the employee is with the company. It needs to be repeated regularly and probably at least annually to take account of changes in working methods and other factors. Where a system of annual appraisal is in place this can certainly be adapted to cover training needs if it does not do so already. However, the assessment can be more informal, including such as a short meeting with an immediate supervisor.

Training records not only provide an up-to-date picture of an employee's training status but also a means of establishing whether identified training needs have been met. There is no point in deciding that someone needs to go on a course if there is no method of checking that this actually happens. Training records do not have to be elaborate; notes in personnel files or lists of attenders at training sessions may be quite sufficient.

Training activities and procedures can be linked into industry schemes, nationally recognised qualifications (eg NVQs) or training standards such as Investors In People (the requirements of this are much more than needed to meet ISO 9000).

PRODUCT IDENTIFICATION AND TRACEABILITY
(4.8)

The requirements of *inspection and test status (4.12)* and *control of nonconforming product (4.13)* – see Chapter 5 – imply a need to identify products. If you cannot be sure which products are nonconforming for example, how can you control them? In the case of physical products, identification may be of unique items (eg a machine) or of batches (you cannot identify a grain of sugar but you can identify the batch). For services with intangible 'products', identification will normally apply to the paperwork raised in performing the service.

There is complete freedom to choose whichever method of identification is appropriate. A numbering system may be devised or even names used if the volume of items concerned is small. The identification may also be applied to the product or associated paperwork in a wide variety of ways – stamping it on, attaching secure labels or plates, tagging etc – whatever is effective for the particular product or business. John Axon of Park Farm number-tags all his cattle except for the bulls which, for good reason, are tattooed (the assessor chose not to go into the bull pen to check this out).

Product identification will usually give some measure of traceability – establishing which processes and which materials went into a particular product. However, depending on the business and product, it may be necessary to be able to trace back to source (ie the supplier and his batch) all inputs going into a product through a far more elaborate record system. This is usually required in businesses with critical safety considerations – eg if a plane crashes it may be essential to check which batch of metal went into the airframe so that other aircraft made from the same material can be examined for potential problems. Where such a requirement exists it will certainly be known through the normal course of business.

Traceability also has other, commercial implications. Datac Adhesives for example is able to trace the materials that have gone into any final products and on occasion, through being able to identify the source of a deficient material, have claimed compensation from the supplier involved – their quality system has in this way led to clearly quantifiable savings. The danger of future product liability claims may also be a reason for having full traceability built into a quality system; possibly claims can be off-loaded on the suppliers which produced the problem in the first place.

CONTROL OF QUALITY RECORDS (4.16)

Many of the requirements of the Standard already discussed mention the need to keep records relating to the operation of the quality system (eg of inspection and testing, supplier assessments etc) and in developing the procedures for a quality system, the need for records, as evidence of compliance with the system and to provide data relating to quality assurance and control, will become apparent. The form of such records can be varied to meet the needs and working practices of the business. Forms, record books, product cards, job files and wall charts are all possibilities. Nor does the record have to be in hard copy; it can be in a computer file which is accessed on screen and this may well be the best approach where computer networks and computer control of production is already well established. However, it may be inadvisable to plan, at the same time, both a quality system and a programme of computerisation.

This specific requirement of ISO 9000 relates to *keeping* quality records rather then when and where they are required. To be of any value, a particular record must be accessible and in a form which is useable. To cover all aspects related to this need, the Standard requires procedures for identification, collection, index-ing, filing, maintenance and disposition of quality records. The need for retrieval and specified retention times are also referred to. The precise methods of meeting all this can be varied to suit the size, complexity and structure of a particular business. The period for which records are kept (specified retention times) should take into account factors such as the expected life of the product, warranty periods, legal requirements, including those that may arise in civil actions, and industry codes. To meet the needs of assessors, the retention period for nearly all quality records is likely to be at least one year but other considerations may well indicate that much longer periods are appropriate.

STATISTICAL TECHNIQUES (4.20)

The inclusion of statistical techniques in ISO 9000 reflects that this is a well established tool in quality assurance and quality improvement programmes. The techniques enable quality levels to be measured and changes plotted and in manufacturing can take the form of statistical process control (SPC). Statistical methods have also been a key methodology of a number of quality gurus and most notably Edward Deming. However, the statistical techniques used in quality systems need not be complicated or devised by a mathematician – a simple running average of reject rates plotted by shift and day is a real application and one which could well help identify causes of problems and suggest solutions. A supplier scoring system as used by Datac Adhesive is another example of the practical application of statistical methods.

This requirement of the Standard includes a need to identify where statistical techniques should be used and there is specific mention of applications for establishing, controlling and verifying process capability and product characteristics – in other words is the process doing what it is supposed to do and does the product match up to requirements? Where statistical techniques are appropriate will vary tremendously and it is possible in some types of business (eg professional services) that no such need can be identified. One factor which may limit their use is the number of comparable measures of a characteristic which are available or can be taken. If over a reasonable time these are few, statistical analysis is not likely to be useful and there is no need to use the techniques just for the sake of doing so (ie to meet the requirement). If it is truly decided that there is no useful application, this is the need identified and the position can be stated in the quality manual. However, see our further comments on the value of statistics and quantification in Chapter 12.

Where statistical techniques are appropriate, procedures are required to define how they will be applied. This may cover the points in the process where the techniques will be used, the data which will be the input into the analysis, the calculation method and who should do the work and interpret the results.

7

Quality System Control Requirements

The remaining five requirements of ISO 9000 all concern managing a formal quality system, see Figure 7.1. As we have already discussed, these requirements are only meaningful in the context of such a system. However, this is not to diminish their importance. Not only will assessors need evidence that all the system control requirements are met but the system cannot work for any time without the mechanisms covered in this part of the Standard.

MANAGEMENT RESPONSIBILITY (4.1)

This requirement includes the need for a quality policy and what an appropriate document should cover is described in the Standard – quality objectives, commitment to quality and the relevance of it to the organisation's own goals and the needs of customers. It is hard to imagine that any business seeking ISO 9000 will find any problem drafting some suitable short document; one page is enough. The policy though must be more than a few well chosen words. For one thing it must be communicated to and understood throughout the company. But above all, the policy must represent real commitment to the quality system by senior management and this need for top level involvement is the sub-text underpinning all of management responsibility. With the increasing pace of registration to ISO 9000, some firms are implementing systems because they feel they have to, but without any real enthusiasm. In such circumstances, senior manage-

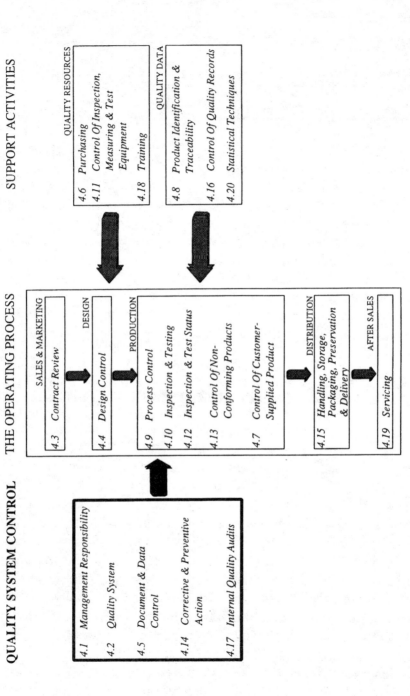

Figure 7.1   Quality system control requirements of ISO 9001

ment often try to off-load the project and let junior staff shoulder the task. This approach simply does not meet the underlying principles of the Standard or quality assurance. At the very least, a management with this attitude will have to seem to go through all the motions of commitment. While they are playing at it they may as well try and do it for real. Without this commitment, certification may be achieved but the benefits will be much less than they could be and over time the system will probably run down.

Apart from the need for a policy, the requirement of management responsibility covers organisation to implement and maintain an effective system and the need for management review. *Organisation (4.1.2)* includes the need to define responsibility and authority for operating the system and all the tasks relating to quality. These arrangements have to be documented. Adequate resources must also be made available by the company's management to operate the system. These will include physical resources such as testing equipment but also staff with the skills and training to carry out all the tasks required by the system including managing it. There is also a requirement for a *management representative (4.1.2.3)* to be appointed. He or she has two specific roles; administrating the system (ensuring the system matches up to the Standard, is successfully implemented and liaising with assessors etc) and reporting to the company's senior management on how the system is operating. The importance of management commitment is further stressed by requiring that the management representative should be of senior management status and, by implication, that the job should not be off-loaded to a mere clerk. Of course, the management representative can delegate specific tasks to other staff but he or she must remain responsible for them. Incidentally the management representative does not have to be called that; quality manager is often the term used and in smaller companies the role may be part of another job title (eg administration director, company secretary) and combined with other responsibilities – all that needs to be done in this respect is to document the arrangements – usually in the quality manual.

The final area of management responsibility and still emphasising the need for senior commitment, is *management review (4.1.3)*. Clearly if management is committed to the quality system they need to regularly consider whether it is working effectively and what needs to be done to remedy any problems. The mechanism for this is a regular management review meeting of the senior management of the company. In smaller businesses this will often be the directors and the meeting can be part of a board meeting. The requirement specifies that the meetings should be at regular and specified intervals (quarterly is probably the minimum) and that records should be kept – eg minutes of the meetings.

QUALITY SYSTEM (4.2)

The whole of ISO 9000 is about quality systems – it provides models for such a system – and this specific requirement concerns the need for the system to be formal and documented. The form of the documented system is left flexible so that it can meet the individual needs of organisations and the specified elements are limited to a reference to a quality manual, which describes how the requirements of ISO 9000 are to be met within the company, and which includes or refers to documented quality procedures. It is also formally stated that the system and its procedures must be effectively implemented. Documented quality systems are the subject of Chapter 8 and little more needs saying here except in relation to quality planning.

The system must incorporate a process of quality planning; *how* the objectives of the quality policy and the quality needs of customers are to be met, in practice, in the business. This process must be documented but this does not necessarily require quality plans as such to be produced. Formal quality plans have a role and particularly to control major changes in methods of working or to cover projects outside the normal run of the business. More will be said about such plans in Chapter 8 but they are by no means needed in every system. Instead of (or as well as) formal quality plans, the process of quality planning can be documented in a number of other ways including through the procedures, in design plans, reports produced as the results of corrective actions (see below) or even in documents which are not normally considered part of a quality system – eg business plans. The need for quality planning is made more explicit in the 1994 version than previous versions of ISO 9000 but arguably all that is really new is a specific need to document the process. How this is interpreted in practice by assessors is a bit uncertain and if it seems a problem area, it may well be worth discussing with the certification body selected to carry out assessment.

DOCUMENT AND DATA CONTROL (4.5)

The twin principles involved here are controlled documentation and controlled change. Uniformity is required in the operation of a quality system. In particular, once procedures are defined and agreed, everyone in the organisation must work to the same procedures whenever they are relevant. All must sing from the same sheet. A documented system is a means of putting procedures into practice and achieving uniformity and except in the smallest business there will need to be a number of copies of the procedure manuals and any other types of instructions. The principle of uniformity, however, will clearly break down if each copy of these documents is not the same. In particular, problems will occur if individual copies are not complete or there are different versions – if I am working off Version 1 but you are using Version 3, it is unlikely that we will both apply the same procedures. Different versions of documents are the result of change and the Standard recognises that quality systems are not fixed for all time and need to be changed to solve problems within the system, in the processes or to meets changes in the environment. However, change to the system needs to be controlled to avoid the problems of a uniform system becoming divergent (eg one department working to the original version and another to the new and revised one).

To meet the need to maintain uniformity and control change, this part of the Standard specifies a number of elements including the overriding need for procedures to cover document control and change. Such procedures have to include defined authority for issuing and changing system documentation, mechanisms so that documents can be checked as the correct version (a master list is mentioned as one possibility) and means of ensuring that procedure manuals etc are available for staff to consult – this normally means a number of copies at various points. Also the withdrawal of obsolete versions.[1]

Document control mainly applies to the documentation created internally as part of the system – eg quality and procedure manuals and the masters of forms etc used in applying the procedures. However, as the Standard makes clear, it also applies to any documents brought in from outside that are required in the operation of the quality system. One example is industry standards or regulations which are to be applied as part of the system and these will be often in the form of publications which are updated and reissued from time to time. A system is needed to ensure that the latest editions are to hand and in use. In practice controlling this can be quite difficult. Incidentally the Standard itself is such a document and anyone seeking registration needs to have on file the latest version of the model being implemented (ie ISO 9001 or 9002). This publication apart, however, which external documents are brought into the system is largely a matter for each company to decide. Often it is decided that suppliers' technical manuals should form part of the system (they may well reduce the need to develop procedures) and this was the case at Benfell Communications where several thousand suppliers' manuals, required to install and service equipment effectively, are kept. The control of this library was an issue at the assessment (it took an unacceptably long time to find a specific manual) and the prob-

---

[1] Obsolete versions can be retained and arguably need to be so that changes can be traced. However, it must be clear that these versions are obsolete.

lem was solved by introducing computerised filing (this would be an overkill in most companies).

A final note on the titling of this requirement – the 'data' part of 'document and data control' is a recognition that systems do not have to be wholly (or even entirely) in hard, paper copy. Computer files, provided they can be practically accessed by those needing them, are an alternative.

CORRECTIVE AND PREVENTIVE ACTION (4.14)

Another principle implicit in the quality system approach is the need to solve problems and, therefore implicitly, include the dynamics of quality improvement. Relevant problems may arise in operating the system itself (eg a procedure proves ineffective), in the process (eg a machine breaks down) or in the product; it is faulty. Such problems may be identified by customers complaining, through audits, in test reports and other records produced through operating the system. The Standard requires that the quality system includes procedures for identifying such problems, investigating their causes and developing solutions to put the matter right. Such a solution may involve a change in the quality system (to deal with an ineffective procedure or introduce a new one to deal with a process problem) but it does not have to – problems may be more people related and need solving by training, including making sure staff fully understand the quality system. Where quality changes are required they must of course involve the procedures relating to document control discussed above.[2]

The 1994 version of ISO 9000 (unlike the previous one) makes a distinction between corrective and preventive actions but in practice this is often only a theoretical matter. The emphasis of corrective actions is to find an immediate solution to a problem – a customer complains about a product and a means of

---

[2] It is good practice to tie in all document changes to corrective action – ie no change can be authorised unless it has been proposed and recommended through the corrective action procedure.

making him happy again is found – whereas preventive actions focus on the longer term – how can similar problems be prevented in future? However, most systems are likely to have a common procedure covering both needs and to build in a means of considering the long term implications of problems firstly requiring an immediate fix.

INTERNAL QUALITY AUDITS (4.17)

Not only is there a requirement to solve problems but they must be positively sought out through a process of internal quality audits. Such audits must be carried out by trained staff (suitable training can be provided internally) who are independent of the area of the business covered in an audit. In practice this may be achieved by having auditors not involved in areas of the business covered by the Standard (eg accounts staff) or use cross auditing where someone working in one department audits another. However it is achieved, independence is needed to ensure audits are thorough and objective.

The Standard specifies a number of elements relating to audit work including: documented procedures to cover the activity, attention in the audit to the working of the quality system and the results it achieves, selection of areas for audit on the basis of their importance, the recording of the results of auditing, using corrective action procedures to deal with any problems found through auditing and a system of follow-ups to establish whether any problems found in the initial audit have been effectively dealt with (through corrective actions).

Someone planning a quality system may well feel initially that auditing appears to be a dull, bureaucratic and even a make-work activity. Done properly it is none of these and is essential for the effective operation of a quality system. Even if auditing was not a requirement of the Standard, any quality system will almost certainly cease to be effective without this important process. Furthermore, internal audits mirror the work of external assessors and prepares a company for assessment. The only difference is that often internal auditors' work is more thorough and 'tougher'. Some of the practicalities of auditing are discussed in Chapter 11.

THE QUALITY TRIANGLE

It should be apparent from this chapter that the quality system control requirements and procedures developed to implement them all closely lock together. The quality triangle illustrated in Figure 7.2 represents this.

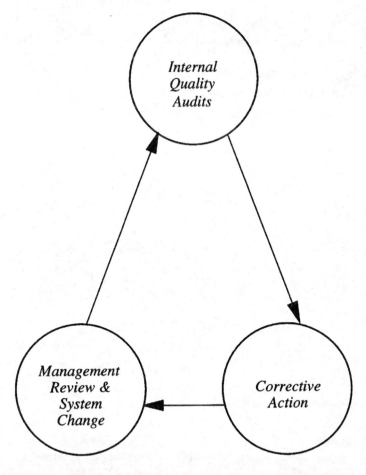

Figure 7.2 The quality triangle

Internal auditing identifies problems in the operation of the quality system. The corrective action procedure then investigates the causes of the problem and recommends a solution. The resulting report is then considered at a management review meeting[3] and if appropriate the system is changed in a controlled way (following the document change procedures) to solve the problem. Later the implementation of this solution is examined by the audit process and if there is still a problem the loop is followed again, and if necessary again and again until the problem is solved – it must be eventually.

As we will repeat later, quality systems, although they must be documented, are not just works of literature. They must be implemented and followed. The mechanisms within the quality triangle, if followed properly, will ensure the system is effective. The only other important aspect of achieving ISO 9000 is ensuring the system covers all the other requirements of the Standard.

---

[3] The system may give an individual (eg the management representative) the authority to make urgent changes before the matter is considered at a review meeting. Also it should be stressed again that the solution to all problems does not have to be a change in the system.

8

Documented Quality Systems

As we discussed in Chapter 7, ISO 9000 requires a formal, documented quality system. What this involves is covered in this chapter. We first discuss the system as a whole and then look in some detail at the key parts.

QUALITY SYSTEMS ARE UNIQUE

An important point is that a quality system has to be unique even though it is developed to match the requirements of the Standard. The system of a solicitor will be very different to that of a ball bearing manufacturer. Moreover, the system of one solicitors' practice will be different in detail to another; because they are different people, working in different places and with different approaches.

First and foremost an effective quality system must meet the quality assurance needs of the individual business almost regardless of whatever ISO 9000 requires. As discussed in Chapter 9, a very large part of the work involved in developing a system is formalising existing practice. New and improved methods of working can be added as the system is developed but in general we cannot recommend this approach – it is far better to make the changes once the system is in place, following the formal methods for change within the system. Of course, we cannot be over-idealistic. An important goal is going to be to achieve ISO 9000 and it is likely that when all existing practice is formalised, some of the requirements of the Standard will not be adequately addressed. For this reason some changes in existing working methods will have to be made. However, it is better to approach building the system in this way and 'back-into' ISO 9000 than working the other way, which is to develop procedures to meet the Standard regardless of existing and established practice.

THE PARTS OF A SYSTEM

Figure 8.1 represents the parts of a quality system to meet ISO 9000. The pyramid structure is apt because the documents in the upper layers are briefer and more general than those in the lower layer. Conversely those in the lower layer are likely to be used more frequently and practically than the documents at the apex of the pyramid, which are of more symbolic importance.

Figure 8.1 The quality system pyramid

Terms in general use in quality assurance are used to describe the parts of the system, but do not be alarmed by them. The quality policy can just as well be called the 'quality statement', the quality manual a 'guide to the quality system' and the procedures 'working methods'. It really does not matter as long as the staff using the system know the terminology and that somewhere there is a translation to the jargon of ISO 9000 (usually in the quality manual or equivalent). Also the parts do not have to be bound separately; eg the quality manual and procedures can be kept together in one volume if you prefer and usually the policy forms part of the manual.

DOCUMENT CONTROL

Document control (or controlled documentation) is a very important principle that must be incorporated into a quality system and the reasons underlying the Standard's requirement for this were discussed in Chapter 7. Three practical tools to achieve control and which apply to a system as a whole, are document lists, circulation lists and controlled/uncontrolled copies.

As discussed earlier, quality systems can be changed and eventually are bound to be, but in a formal and controlled way. This results in different and later versions of documents and especially procedures being issued. A document list simply shows for each separate and identified document the latest version reference (eg version 3) and the date it was issued. Every time a new version is issued the list is updated. The level of documentation identified in the list, is the level at which changes are made in practice – in the case of the quality manual this may be the whole document (it is fairly short and generally not changed often) but for procedures it is likely to be a group of them linked by relating to some stage in the process (eg the specimen corrective action procedures at the end of this chapter would be changed as a whole rather than by individual paragraphs etc).

A circulation list is simply an index of each controlled copy of a document, showing where it is kept and who is in charge of it.

In a small company an appropriate number of copies of the procedure manual is normally in single figures and, therefore, the list can be short. An important point about the number of controlled copies is that control is easier to maintain if there are fewer rather than many. However, the converse of this is that there must be enough copies so that staff can consult them, but this does not have to mean one per person.

Controlled copies of manuals are those which you can be sure are complete and up to date and therefore covered by the control process. It is essential that only such controlled copies are *used* within the company – if staff refer to and work from uncontrolled copies (eg ones they have copied themselves) there can be no guarantee that these are complete and up to date. Uncontrolled copies can be kept providing they are not 'in use' although why should these be needed at all? One superseded copy of a procedure is likely to be kept for formal record purposes. However, uncontrolled copies can be sent outside the organisation (eg the quality manual or policy to customers). In fact any copies which are sent outside must be uncontrolled because you have lost any capacity to control them. It is useful to make controlled copies visually distinctive – eg printing them on special paper, stamping each page 'controlled' in red etc. It is then obvious if any uncontrolled copies are around.

QUALITY POLICY

The quality policy is the shortest document in the system; one page or less is quite adequate. As discussed in Chapter 7, the Standard specifies elements which must be covered in the statement but the really important requirement is that it symbolises a *real* commitment. A specimen policy statement is attached at the end of this chapter and this illustrates what is needed, although it can be expressed in many different ways. The statement defines the company's quality objective and its commitment to it and links this to customer needs and the wider goals of the business. Reference is also made to the Standard and a formal quality system. Finally the commitment of staff is stated as well as that the policy has been made by the company's management.

The quality policy is normally bound in the quality manual but is also often displayed around the premises since staff are expected to know it – not word for word, parrot fashion but be able to express the key concepts in their own words. Assessors may well test whether staff understand the policy. The policy can also be used as a marketing tool; in brochures, attached to quotations or even carried by the salesforce.

QUALITY MANUAL

A quality manual (however titled) is a formal requirement of the Standard. Its key purpose is to state and particularly for the benefit of assessors, how the requirements of ISO 9000 are met in the company's own quality system and reference the link to other parts of the system – especially the procedures. The following extract from a quality manual illustrates what we mean:

4.14 Corrective And Preventive Action

4.14.1 General

Problems arising from the processes carried out or from the operation of the Quality System, whether identified by audit or other staff or through customer complaint, shall be investigated, analysed and corrective and preventive actions recommended and authorised through formal Procedures (see Procedures 11.4). These procedures also cover the documentation of corrective actions.

4.14.2 Corrective Action

4.14.3 Preventive Action

The distinction between corrective and preventive action is recognised but the Procedures use 'corrective action' to cover both requirements.

In the example, a statement is made on how the requirements for corrective and preventive action are to be met. The headings in italics are as per the Standard. A cross reference is given to the procedures for corrective action which tell the staff concerned *how* to carry out corrective actions – clearly the statement alone lacks enough detail for uniform implementation. A note is also made on the terminology used in procedures – that 'corrective action' includes the concepts of both corrective and preventive action (as per the Standard).

All the other requirements of the Standard can be covered in exactly the same way and together make up the large part of the quality manual. The complete contents may include those listed and discussed below although there is scope for considerable variation.

EXAMPLE OF QUALITY MANUAL STRUCTURE

Frontpiece
Foreword
Circulation
Background To The Company
Company Quality Policy
Scope Of The Quality System
Company Organisation
Description Of The Quality System

Briefly, the elements of the structure of the quality manual set out above, are as follows. The *frontpiece* would include the title and control information (eg version number, date of issue and that the particular copy is controlled and is copy number 1 etc). The *foreword* can be little more than a statement of what the document is (ie the quality manual of the company) and perhaps a clarification of the availability of controlled and uncontrolled copies. The *circulation* is the list of all controlled copies and their location. The *background* to the company is for the benefit of those who are not familiar with it – a paragraph or two would suffice although if the quality manual is to be used as a marketing tool some puffery may be appropriate. The *company quality policy* is self explanatory – a copy of that statement. The *scope of the quality system* can formally link it to the Standard (eg 'implemented to the requirements of BS/EN/ISO 9001') and indicate that the system applies to the whole of the company and its operations (or if this is not the case, to which parts it does apply). A reference might also be made to the other elements of the system and especially the procedures (the main headings of these might be listed together with their reference numbers). *Company organisation* is again for the benefit of those unfamiliar with the business and can usefully include charts showing, in broad terms[1], both the organisational structure (the hierarchy) and the processes of the company. Finally the *description of the quality system* can be best set out as suggested above – each of the Standard's headings followed by a statement of how they are implemented.

All staff should be aware that the quality manual exists and it should be reasonably accessible. However, the quality manual is not a guide to day to day action and it is unrealistic to expect most staff to read it in full detail. The senior management, the management representative and others involved in administrating the quality system, however, should have a much greater familiarity with this document. It is also very important in the assessment since it provides a bridge between the Standard (which the assessor knows) and a company's own quality system (which the assessor does not know). In this respect, the cross referencing of procedures is particularly useful. Finally the quality manual can be used as a marketing tool and sent to selected customers including those asking for details of quality assurance (eg as part of their own review of suppliers). In these cases it is of course *uncontrolled* copies (marked as such) which are sent out.

PROCEDURES

Procedures are at the heart of the quality system. They are the documents which tell staff how to follow a quality system, day to

---

[1] We would advise against too much detail here since when the organisation or the processes change the quality manual may have to be up-dated for this reason alone. Do not use individuals' names – they will be sure to have moved on before the ink is dry.

day, in their own work. Before reading any further it will be useful to look at the specimen procedure bound at the end of this chapter. This will show what a procedure (or group of procedures – the line between the singular and plural really does not matter) looks like. The one included is for corrective actions – a procedure in some form or other required in all systems and which has been used for this reason (whereas one for the burnishing of right-handed grommets or of any other specific production process would be of more limited interest).

Procedures describe *how* to carry out quality related activities and, therefore, go beyond the broad statements contained in the quality manual. Contrast the quality manual extract on page 99 with the specimen procedure. Both concern corrective action but whilst the quality manual extract expresses an intention to meet a requirement of the Standard, nobody could use this as a practical guide (if several people tried the results would be quite different in detail). The procedure, however, describes step by step what has to be done. It might be objected that even the procedure misses out some important things – eg how investigations are to be carried out – but there is a logic here which we shall discuss shortly.

Effective procedures should embody four principles and these should be kept in mind when drafting them.

FOUR PRINCIPLES OF EFFECTIVE PROCEDURES

1. Understandable
2. Actionable
3. Auditable
4. Mandatory

Procedures are to be followed and, therefore, they must be capable of being understood by the staff who are to follow them. The ability of staff to read and understand instructions will vary through an organisation and it is recommended that procedures should be drafted with the least able reader in mind – they should, therefore, use the simplest language, short sentences and avoid dense blocks of text.

It may seem obvious that procedures should be actionable but it is quite easy to write high sounding ones which cannot be followed in practice – perhaps the conditions assumed are not present or another step in the process does not happen in the way implied. Even with the greatest care, a complete system written from scratch will almost certainly contain, in early versions, procedures which are not actionable.

Procedures should also be auditable. In other words there should be some evidence *after the event* that the procedure has been followed (or not). This is not simply a matter of making life easy for the internal auditors. If a procedure cannot be audited it is no more than an expression of good intentions. So why have it there at all? Setting out intentions is not the purpose of procedures.

The final principle is that procedures are mandatory. Any staff involved in the process covered by the procedure must follow that procedure. Quite possibly they may consider that the procedure is an absolutely ridiculous way of carrying out the activity and that they know a method which is ten times better. Fine. Let them use the corrective action procedure to suggest and have approved their superior approach. But until this is done and the documented procedure changed in the formal way, they must be expected to follow 'the book'. Staff not following procedures should be trained to do so. Ultimately some may need disciplining if they wilfully disregard the system. If this is not acceptable to the company's culture – and it may not be – the company should almost certainly not be seeking ISO 9000 registration. By extension, it is recommended to leave out of procedures any possibility that a procedure need not be followed or is semi-optional. Phrases such as 'it is preferable' or 'it is good practice wherever possible' should be left out. If something to be done is to be left to discretion (and this may be appropriate) then it should not be included in the procedures.

It is also useful to consider what are not procedures. Firstly procedures are not an exhaustive description of all activities or detail every step in a process – only those activities which are relevant to the quality of the product need to be covered. In an engineering works for example, changing the tool on a press may be a complex job requiring many hours work by a skilled fitter. However, quite possibly, the tool can only be attached satisfactorily or not and in the latter case the process will just not work and the quality of the output not compromised (though scheduling might be disrupted). In such a case it may be enough to state in the procedures that 'the specified tool shall be fitted to the press'.[2] A second point is that procedures or procedure manuals are not training manuals – it is assumed that the staff operating the process, covered by a procedure, are trained to do the job. In the specimen procedure someone is appointed to investigate a deficiency. But how are they expected to do this? The answer is that staff trained and capable of this task are given the job. This point is in a way obvious because the alternative is wholly impractical. Someone walking in off the street cannot practise as a solicitor by following a procedure manual and to attempt to make this possible would require a document that encompasses all law. However, procedure manuals and quality systems generally do have a link to training since they provide a framework around which training programmes can be developed – P&O European Ferries, for example, found this an important benefit of the whole ISO 9000 process. Also, procedure manuals can be very useful in inducting a new recruit who is technically trained and competent but unfamiliar with the company's practice.

Procedures are required to cover all the processes and activities of a business or at least those relevant to ISO 9000. With the implementation of a quality system these also have to include those relating to quality system control (as identified in Chapter 7). To be effective, specific procedures should be developed for each step in the process – several shorter procedures covering bits

---

[2] Even if faulty fitting of the tool could lead to product defects, an alternative to writing a procedure may be to reference the press supplier's handbook, although note that in this case the latter should be treated as a controlled document.

of the process usually work better than one long one for a major chunk of the operation. It is also recommended that each procedure follows the structure of the process and includes all the quality activities needed for that process. This might for example, describe the process, specify tests carried out during or after the process and describe what happens if a product is found to be faulty. Using this approach a procedure may, therefore, address several separate requirements of the Standard (and each requirement may be covered in a number of procedures). An alternative approach, but one we cannot recommend, is to take each of the headings or sub-headings of the Standard (eg *inspection and testing (4.10)*) and develop a procedure to implement it. What is wrong with this approach is that such procedures are difficult to follow in practice – the operator in the press shop for example may need to check several quite disparate procedures to carry out a simple task (in practice he will simply give up and not read them at all). The exception to this is, however, some of the Standard's requirements relating to support activities and quality system control – in the case of the latter at least, it is probably best to have a procedure relating to each requirement (eg as per the specimen procedure for corrective action at the end of this chapter).

In developing procedures, a major problem is getting the balance of detail right. On the one hand all the steps that affect quality must be covered and all the requirements of the Standard met. However, the longer the documentation, the harder it will be to follow (and the less likely that it will be followed). The only real guide is good judgement but where in doubt it is usually better to go for the minimum rather than maximum.

Finally, there is the question of the layout and collation of procedures. The format should be to a standard so that users recognise them as procedures and are familiar with their sequence and layout. Precisely what format is used is unimportant. The one used for the specimen procedure is only one possibility (short explanatory notes on the format used follow the procedure). Procedures also need keeping in some order and together and a common approach is in a loose-leaf binder with a circulation and

document list at the front. In smaller companies it is usually better to have the required number of such binders (eg one per department) containing identical sets of procedures. However, in larger businesses it may be better to make available, at each point, just those procedures that apply there, although with this approach, document control is often more difficult. The sequence of procedures within a binder will follow the numbering system used and it is preferable if this has some logic (eg with at least those relating to the operating process mirroring the sequence of the operation). However, there is no requirement for this in the Standard – they can just be in the order in which they are written.

The documented procedures in use within a company must of course be controlled versions. Uncontrolled versions can be sent outside the organisation but this is usually neither neccesary nor desirable.

QUALITY PLANS AND WORKS INSTRUCTIONS

Although quality planning is a requirement of ISO 9000, this process does not have to be recorded in documents labelled 'quality plans'. In Chapter 7 we suggested some alternatives. Quality plans are, however, often an effective approach, including in the following circumstances:

○ Where the business involves very large and unique orders or projects. Manufacturers of major capital equipment, civil engineering and long term consultancy programmes are all examples.

○ For a product or project which is substantially different to the normal range of activities.

○ When developing a new product range.

○ If making significant changes to the processes which will substantially affect the quality of the final product.

Quality plans may also form part of the contract with the customer – the customer requires a quality plan to be prepared for the order. This is likely to include arrangements for customer inspection and testing. However, this is only likely to be required in the type of large scale project businesses where quality plans would be appropriate in any case.

The purpose of quality plans is to show how the quality objectives and policy is to be applied in a particular case; for a large order, a new product or to changes in the process. They therefore relate a general quality system to particular circumstances. Because they are for unique circumstances, it is difficult to give more specific advice on writing and formatting these documents but one approach may be to go back to the Standard and describe how its requirements (or the relevant ones) will be met in the particular case. This will produce the counterpart of the quality manual which describes how the Standard will be met in a particular business (rather than in a particular project). A quality plan, however, is additional to and not a substitute for a quality manual, or for that matter procedures. Where the regular use of quality plans is anticipated, their application should be mentioned in the quality manual (ie under the heading *quality planning (4.2.3)*) and the arrangements for initiating and authorising a plan covered in the procedures.

If quality plans apply to special projects, works instructions are the opposite – they are used for standard products. They are best thought of as recipes specifying how a particular product or model is to be produced, eg the ingredients and processes for one adhesive. Works instructions are really, therefore, detailed procedures. General procedures will describe and control the operations of a department but works instructions relate these to individual products passing through the department.

Works instructions are not a specific requirement of ISO 9000 and whether or not they are useful must be decided in each case. In a 'jobbing' type of business, where each product is different, standard works instructions will probably be inappropriate[3] and

---

[3] In jobbing businesses the term work instructions may be used for the document which passes from sales to the works and specifies what is to be done to meet the order. However, this is rather different to the general type of work instructions discussed above.

even where standard product ranges are produced, the general procedures may be quite adequate without going to the trouble of writing seperate works instructions for each product. However, this approach to quality system documentation can be useful and possibly reduce the need for, or the length of, more general procedures. Works instructions must of course be treated as controlled documentation and linked into other parts of the quality system (eg identified in related procedures).

QUALITY RECORDS

More than anything else, forms are what give ISO 9000 a bad name. Too often the result of implementing the Standard is seen to be an explosion of form filling. Strictly speaking there is *no* requirement in the Standard to produce and fill in forms. What is required is records. As mentioned in the previous chapters, some requirements of ISO 9000 do require quality records to be kept (eg including those relating to contract review, design, inspection and testing and purchasing). Also, as we have argued earlier in this chapter, effective procedures should be auditable and often (but not always) this will require some record to be made.

For records kept in a paper/hard copy format, forms ought to make record keeping easier than the alternative of free-form note taking. In some circumstances, free-form records may be the most effective approach (eg farmer John Axon keeps some important records on boards kept near his animals) but generally they give rise to problems of inconsistent, incomplete or just illegible records. Well designed forms should overcome these sorts of problems. The initial versions need to be designed as part of the work of preparing procedures and the linkage between the form and relating procedure should be documented. In the specimen procedure at the end of this chapter, it will be seen that the use of the form is specified in the relating procedure and, to assist identification, the forms are numbered to corre-spond to a procedure (eg the Corrective Action Form is numbered 11.4.1/1 and its use is first mentioned in procedure 11.4.1). In completing a form or other record, there is often a need to identify the individual product or batch to which the record relates and there is a link-up here with the methods used for product identification (which should be spelt out at some point in a procedure).

Forms must be treated as controlled documents. In particular it is essential to ensure that blank copies of the form are available where they are used and that these copies are up to date; the latest version. As time goes on, forms will certainly need amending, either because the relating procedure is changed or because a change in design makes the form easier to use. When such a change is made, it is important that old copies are withdrawn and the new versions substituted. Version numbers on the forms will make control easier and this and other mechanisms to ensure adequate 'document control' should be spelt out in a relevant procedure (probably one specifically addressing the important issue of overall document control).

An alternative to either forms or free-form notes is records kept on computer files. This can be particularly effective where the business is already computerised through networking and the like. Where processes are computer controlled, effective records may be generated automatically onto the files. Computer records must of course be accessible to auditors or assessors (it is acceptable that they may need assistance to access them) but there is no need to produce hard copy just for the purposes of a quality system. On-screen access is quite adequate. Methods of ensuring adequate back-up of computer files must, however, exist and possibly include off-site archiving.

However, returning to the initial point made in this section, an in-built danger of quality systems is form proliferation and substituting computer files or for that matter free-form notes is no solution. Positive action is required to limit record keeping to that which is necessary and no more. Hard thought and good planning are the real solutions but here are a few suggestions for combating the disease of form proliferation:

WAYS OF KEEPING FORMS IN CHECK

1. Make one form cover the records needed for several procedures.

2. When designing the system, consider using methods of record keeping which are already established.

3. Where documents are produced as an intrinsic part of the process (eg in professional services) consider whether these can provide some of the quality system records.

4. Having designed a quality system, review it with the specific objective of reducing the forms and record keeping. Set a target – say 20% fewer forms.

5. Repeat this review annually.

6. More radically, tackle the problem of too many forms by critically questioning the procedures. Is each procedure really needed?

Quality system records need to be kept securely (as discussed in Chapter 6, this is a requirement of the Standard – *control of quality records (4.16)*) and procedures are needed to address issues such as the methods of filing, retention periods etc. These can be set out in procedures specifically relating to this subject or embedded in other procedures. One important decision to make is where are the records to be kept? The main options are filing them at their point of use (eg in the department making the records) or centrally. Either approach (or some of each method) can be effective although as a general rule, central filing may work best in 'jobbing' businesses (possibly with a job file following each project through all processes) and point of use filing in long run production processes. Again the arrangements – and the responsibilities for filing – should be specified in the procedures.

Specimen Document

QUALITY POLICY

It is the objective of Ashton-Jackson & Company to achieve the highest standards of quality in their work.

This objective is necessary in order to meet the needs of customers and to achieve the Company's goal of being a leading and profitable supplier of business books.

In order to meet the objectives of this policy, Ashton-Jackson & Company have implemented a formal and documented quality system to meet the requirements of BS/EN/ISO 9001.

The Company and its management is fully committed to this policy and to its quality system.

All staff are required to be familiar with the policy and to follow all quality system procedures relevant to their work.

This policy was formally adopted by a resolution of the Board of Ashton-Jackson & Company dated January 1st 1995.

Peter Davids
Chairman

Specimen Document

PROCEDURE 11.4
CORRECTIVE ACTION

Purpose
To define procedures to ensure that deficiencies in the Quality System or processes are investigated, corrected and recurrence prevented.

Scope
All parts of the Quality System and processes carried out.

References
Procedure Manual – 11.1 11.2

Definitions
Customer Complaint Negative or unfavourable comments of a specific and substantial content, on the performance of the Company's services, made in any form, by a customer.

Documentation
11.4.1/1 Corrective Action Form
11.4.2/1 Corrective Action Register

Procedures
11.4.1 *Initiation Of A Corrective Action*
Any member of staff identifying a deficiency in the Quality System, its implementation, in the processes covered, or receiving a customer complaint shall initiate a Corrective Action by requesting a Corrective Action Form – 11.4.1/1 – from the Quality Manager.

Additionally, any member of staff may initiate a Corrective Action if he or she believes that improvements can be made to the Quality System or processes.

11.4 V3 1/1/95 QM 1/3

11.4.2 *Issue Of A Corrective Action Form*
On receiving a request as above, the Quality Manager, if (s)he considers the action to be appropriate, shall issue to the initiator a Corrective Action Form – 11.4.1/1 – which shall have a number written on it to correspond to the next sequential form number in the Corrective Action Register – 11.4.2/1.

The Quality Manager shall, on issuing a Corrective Action Form – 11.4.1/1 – make appropriate entries in the Corrective Action Register – 11.4.2/1.

11.4.3 *Statement Of Deficiency*
The initiator shall complete the relevant part of the Corrective Action Form – 11.4.1/1 – and state the nature of the deficiency.

The initiator shall return the Form to the Quality Manager who shall make appropriate entries in the Corrective Action Register – 11.4.2/1.

11.4.4 *Investigation Of The Deficiency*
The Quality Manager shall appoint a member of staff (s)he considers suitable, to investigate the causes of the deficiency and to make a recommendation on whether a change to the Quality System is required and if so the nature of the change. The investigator may also or instead make a recommendation on the implementation of the Quality System including any requirement for staff training.

The Quality Manager shall pass to the investigator the relevant Corrective Action Form – 11.4.1/1 and make appropriate entries in the Corrective Action Register – 11.4.2/1.

The investigator shall record the results of the investigation on the Corrective Action Form – 11.4.1/1 and pass the Form, with the relevant parts completed, back to the Quality Manager.

11.4 V3 1/1/95 QM 2/3

11.4.5 *Referral Or Action By The Quality Manager*

The Quality Manager, as (s)he considers appropriate, shall either take action in relation to the Corrective Action or refer the matter to the next Management Review Meeting (see 11.1).

In either case, the decision (action by the Quality Manager or referral) shall be recorded on the Corrective Action Form – 11.4.1/1 and in the Corrective Action Register – 11.4.2/1.

11.4.6 *Management Decision*

The Quality Manager or a Management Review Meeting shall then review the Corrective Action and decide:

To make changes to the Quality System either as proposed by the investigator or otherwise. Such a change shall be made through the Document Control procedure – 11.2

Or

To make no change to the Quality System but, if appropriate, take action on the implementation of the Quality System with due regard to any training requirements.

The Quality Manager shall record this decision on the relevant Corrective Action Form – 11.4.1/1 – and in the Corrective Action Register – 11.4.2/1.

11.4.7 *Retention Of Records*

The Quality Manager shall be responsible for keeping all records relating to Procedures 11.4 and retain them for a minimum period of five years after which they may be destroyed.

11.4 V3 1/1/95 QM 3/3

Corrective Action Form No.		

1. STATEMENT OF DEFICIENCY

....
....
....
....

Signed:.. (Person Reporting Deficiency)   Date:..............

2. INVESTIGATION REPORT

No Change Recommended ( )   Change Recommended as Below ( )

....
....
....
....

Signed:.. (Investigator)   Date:..............

3.   REFERRAL/QUALITY MANAGER ACTION

Referral ( )   QM Action ( )

4.   PROCEDURAL CHANGE DECISION

Implement Investigator's Recommendations ( )   No Change ( )

Other Changes - As Below

....
....
....
....

5.   DATE OF CHANGE IMPLEMENTATION (IF RELEVANT)

11.4.2/1   Corrective Action Register   V1

Form No	Date Issued	Issued To	Brief Description of Deficiency	Date Returned	Investigator	Date to Invest	Date Returned	Referral/ QM Action	Procedure Change Decision	Date of Implementation (If Relevant)

NOTES ON THE FORMAT OF THE SPECIMEN PROCEDURE

Number And Title. (Procedure 11.4 – Corrective Action). This is for identification purposes and for cross referencing to other procedures or in the quality manual. You do not *have* to use numbers but it would be very inconvenient not to do so.

Purpose. This is so anyone reading the procedure knows quickly the point of it. Incidentally, writing out the purpose is a help in drafting a procedure – if you cannot describe this simply something is wrong.

Scope. Where in the organisation the procedure applies. In this case the procedure applies across the whole of the quality system but others might apply to one department – eg dispatch.

Reference. Other procedures or parts of the quality system which the user of the procedure may need to refer to. This is a tidy approach but definitely not essential.

Definitions. Any term, the meaning of which might not be clear to the users of the procedures, should be defined. It might be thought that 'customer complaint' is not something that needs defining. However, there can be room for doubt about when a mere comment becomes a complaint. There should not be too many definitions (avoid jargon as much as possible in the first place). Some assessors consider that definitions should be included for their benefit but this often seems unreasonable – the business may use all sorts of technical terms but if these are well understood in the organisation, providing lots of definitions does not serve any useful purpose.

Documentation. The forms used in carrying out the procedure – copies are also attached at the end of the procedure and listing them here is an aid in checking that the procedure is complete and helps auditors or the assessor.

Procedure. The meat of the whole thing – what staff have to actually do. In this case the responsibilities for carrying out tasks are defined in the text but could, instead, be set out under a separate heading.

Plating. The mysterious code at the bottom of the page. The purpose of this is to assist in document control (checking that the procedure is complete and the latest version). It can be cryptic because its interest is largely to such as auditors rather than everyday users. In this example '11.4' identifies the procedure (again), 'V3' is the version number, 'QM' is the authority for issue (the Quality Manager) and '1/3' '2/3' etc is the page number and the number of pages in the whole set – to check if it is all there.

9

Developing a System

Chapter 8 outlined what is required for a documented quality system meeting ISO 9000. This chapter is about getting there – how to develop the system. Some topics covered include: managing and planning the project, sources of help and advice, planning procedures and writing them and the other documents needed to comply with the Standard.

PROJECT PLANNING AND MANAGEMENT

ISO 9000 will be a major project for any company. It will require commitment and considerable effort by staff at all levels. The external or explicit costs alone will not be inconsequential. For many businesses it will also be a very new type of experience and involve change in many areas. Bearing all this in mind, it is surprising how many companies seeking ISO 9000 do not approach the task as a planned project. The consequence is that often the whole process takes far longer than necessary and is less successful than it might have been in the benefits achieved.

The first requirement of a successful project is commitment. This has already been discussed in relation to having a system at all and is equally essential in all the work of creating it. Company-wide commitment is needed at all levels, but especially among senior management who must expect to be involved in the project from beginning to end. Some consultants specialising in quality systems, will not take on a client if the chief executive of the company does not show the right sort of commitment and willingness to make time available for the project.

The project leader also needs to be from or near the top of the company since authority is essential to take the project through to a successful conclusion, regardless of all the other concerns, whether day to day or longer term, which must also be attended to. Often a balance has to be struck between the goal of achieving ISO 9000 and the need to keep business coming in. Having the 'gong' is worthless if the price is a serious decline in day to day revenue earning business as a result of managers diverting their focus and attention. This requires judgement and the decision-making authority of a senior member of staff. The choice of project leader should be made at board level. In small companies there often is no real choice and one person is clearly going to lead the project; in very small businesses this will nearly always be the boss, for example the case at Benfell Communications where managing director Michael Leigh was very much involved in all the detail of the system. Where there is a real choice to be made, there is a paradox which should influence the decision – anyone with a significant amount of time available to head the project is probably a bad choice; he or she is probably available because they are not competent (or no longer so) for the core activities of the company – they are a 'dead elephant'. The principle of delegation may, however, overcome this problem and enable someone who 'has not the time' to successfully manage and oversee the project. Anyone suitable as project manager must be able to delegate.

If the management team as a whole is to be truly committed to the project, they must clearly be kept informed of its progress. An effective device to ensure this is to hold regular management review meetings (discussed in Chapters 7 and 10) right from the start, with the project manager reporting on progress and any problems or inputs required discussed. Another aspect of this approach is that often the project manager will become (like it or not) the management representative (however titled) once the system is up and running. Therefore, the mechanism for effective management review is put in place from the start. However, the project leader does not have to take on this other role; others may be better qualified. The skills and temperament needed to develop a system are not always the same as those needed to run it.

As already suggested, commitment must exist among all layers of staff and not just at the top. The key in this respect is communication. Once a decision is made to seek ISO 9000, everyone should be told of what is involved including the likely timetable – the managers should market the project internally. As much as anything, this is needed to correct misconceptions and allay suspicions. Initially attitudes can be hostile – at Kent County Council Highways and Transportation, for example, there was an initial feeling that the whole thing was unnecessary ('we are the best, so why do we need a system?') and some fear that the result would be staff efforts dissipated in useless paperwork. Such feelings need to be addressed, and the methods are less critical than sucessfully communicating the importance attached to involvement. This is the key to positive attitudes. If staff are truly involved in developing a system how can they really criticise it? Also, involvement is needed to produce an effective system, particularly when it comes to drafting the procedures.

Involving the staff and communication is, therefore, part of the initial planning carried out by a project manager. Other tasks at this stage are planning the resources needed for the project, preparing a timetable and getting a budget together.

The resources needed are nearly all people. A list of the staff who should work on the project needs preparing and their involvement at least pencilling-in on the timetable. Obviously they should also be briefed on what they are to do and when. Another type of people-related resource is bringing in expertise; either consultants or in other forms – this is discussed shortly. Only trivial physical resources are usually required, except possibly in the area of measuring and testing equipment which may need bringing up to scratch. Otherwise it is a matter of modest printing costs and other stationery, although if the company has no word processor now is definitely the time to invest in one.

The timetable should set completion dates for the main stages of the work, which after the initial planning, are: process analysis, review, procedure development and writing and preparing all the final documentation. Each of these steps is discussed in this chapter. The longest time will be procedure development and drafting and it is here that slippage is most likely. Timetables should be firm commitments but not sacrosanct; some flexibility will be needed but hopefully not too much. Incidentally one benefit a consultant might bring is to strengthen deadlines – it concentrates the mind if a consultant is to charge £500 for a day's visit which will be wasted if agreed work has not been done by the internal team.

In setting a timetable, some sense is needed of what is a reasonable period from the start of the project to implementation. This will vary tremendously between companies, depending on a host of factors. Our case study companies generally took between six and twelve months to build their systems and this sort of period is fairly typical. Given enough resources – and this means people's time – it is probably possible to develop a system for a small company in two or three weeks. But this is assuming the staff do little else and if there is so much slack in the business it is probably going downhill so fast that there will be more urgent priorities than ISO 9000. At the other end of the scale, the project can last for several years but this is equally unsatisfactory – staff interest and commitment will start to evaporate after a year.

A budget is needed for the project and should be set at the outset. The costs are both explicit and implicit. The explicit costs include consultants' fees (if they are used), the cost of other forms of bought-in expertise, assessment charges and a small allowance for such as printing etc. In the next section we consider the costs of consultants and in Chapter 11 the charges made for assessment. These need realistically estimating and the necessary finance secured. The implicit costs are all to do with staff time spent on the project. Generally this is not measured or costed but, at least in theory, there is an opportunity cost incurred in diverting staff from more direct and short-term revenue activities. In practice, these costs are often very hard to measure, not only because there is no system in place to track activities in this way but the time spent on the project is somehow squeezed in at the expense of leisure or by doing other things more efficiently – no bad by-product of the project.

CONSULTANTS AND OTHER SOURCES OF EXPERTISE

The first point to make about ISO 9000 consultants is that they are by no means essential. In fact none of the case study organisations employed independent consultants. If expertise is lacking (and it probably is in an ISO 9000 project) there are other ways of bringing it in apart from by using consultants. However, the major argument in favour of consultants is that this is an effective route to buying in knowledge and especially about the requirements of the Standard and its application. The practical value of this expertise is guidance; there are real dangers of going off at a tangent and developing a system which is either impractical or simply does not meet the Standard. Also, without expert guidance, the system may end up over-elaborate and far more than is truly required.

Another potential benefit of consultants is that they are outsiders and can look at an organisation with fresh eyes, not kowtow to the local idols and have nothing to lose by dispelling illusions. However, these benefits depend on a certain open-mindedness by the client company. Consultants can also take on specific tasks required in building a quality system – drafting the quality manual is a good example – and where the skills and experience of a consultant may enable the job to be done more efficiently than by internal staff. However, there is also a danger here. Consultants should be primarily facilitators and not doers. The quality system must be the company's and not the consultant's and this necessitates that most of the work that goes into it has to be from internal staff. There are 'consultants' around, who, after a short briefing, will sit in a corner and draft a full quality system. The result may just get the company through ISO 9000 but will otherwise be no good. Without considerable involvement by staff, the system will not be 'owned' and consequently not effectively implemented.

Consultants will offer full programmes of work, taking the client through the whole process of system development, implementation and up to the point of assessment. The now defunct Dti Quality Initiative was built around this and involved a consultant input of 15 days' work (for smaller companies). Such a full scale commission can be effective, but consultants can also be used in other ways and with a much smaller (and cheaper) involvement; from one day's work upwards. A 'mini' consultancy programme might cover a day spent doing a review (see below), another making recommendations on an overall plan of the procedures and a third and final day testing the finished system. Such a package could be a very effective way of assisting the work of internal staff and may cost less than many training courses.

There is no shortage of quality and ISO 9000 consultants to choose from if it is decided this form of assistance is needed. The choice ranges from independent freelances up to the largest partnerships of management consultants, with a corresponding range of fees from £200 or less per day up to £1000 per day. Independent consultants range in ability and skills from the abysmal to excellent. There are also variations within and between larger consultancy firms but probably more guarantee of minimum standards and of course a greater range of resources to draw on, including a replacement if the lead consultant falls ill (always a potential problem with the independent consultant). The main skill which should be sought in any consultant is experience of successfully implementing quality systems and a good understanding of ISO 9000. It is also generally better to use one who has applied these skills in your own industry (or a closely related one). Not only will a consultant with this experience have a working grasp of the processes involved in the business but is more likely to be able to relate and interpret the requirements of the Standard.

Sources for finding consultants include the IQA[1] and AQMC[2] – bodies which may provide lists of possibly suitable consultants, trade associations for the relevent industry and local TECs (Training and Enterprise Councils). After an initial meeting, a consultant should be expected to provide, at no cost, written terms of reference setting out what work will be done and how. A timetable and firm costing should also be provided.

TECs may not only be able to suggest qualified consultants, they may offer some funding towards the costs of ISO 9000 implementation, or at least advice on the availability of other grants and schemes. There is some variation between the assistance offered and packages from each TEC and early contact is strongly recommended. TECs also provide training programmes linked to quality assurance and ISO 9000. There are as well numerous commercial organisations running courses and seminars on ISO 9000 or specific aspects of quality management (eg procedure writing, auditing etc). Then there are the less formal (and less expensive) methods of acquiring the expertise, including self learning training packages such as from the Sunday Times Business Skills series, books – not least of course this one – and talking to managers in other companies who have gone through the process. Finally there is the experience of new recruits to a company who may have been involved in ISO 9000 systems elsewhere. Bringing in a new and experienced member of staff to take on the role of project leader (and possibly other functions) might also be a possibility although their lack of familiarity with the company may be a handicap.

---

[1] IQA – Institute of Quality Assurance, PO Box 712, 61 Southwark Street, London, SE1 1SB. Tel. 0171 401 2988. The IQA's publication *Quality World* is a useful source of information including about quality related training courses.

[2] AQMC – Association of Quality Management Consultants, 4 Beyne Road, Olivers Battery, Winchester, Hants, SO22 4JW. Tel. 01962 864394.

PROCESS ANALYSIS

After arranging how the project is to be managed, drawing up a timetable and deciding on the resources needed, we recommend that the first step towards developing a quality system should be to analyse the process. Arguably, this is not absolutely essential but with this approach the final system is more likely to be logical and well thought out. Moreover, except in very large organisations, good analysis is more a matter of quality of input than quantity; it does not need to involve many man-hours.

Figure 9.1 should make clear what we mean by process analysis. It is a pictorial representation of what happens in the business – how an order is turned into a delivery. Each box in the chart represents a major stage in the process and, like Russian dolls, can be opened up to look at the sub-processes involved. This more detailed analysis will be required later, but at this stage the process only needs to be shown in this summary or high level form. A process chart such as in the figure is quite different to one showing the organisation and hierarchy (the boss at the top, the works cat at the bottom and the various departments in between). Possibly there will be some overlap between process 'boxes' and departments but not necessarily so – in the example 'design' might be carried out in several different areas and departments. The current organisation and hierarchy is not irrelevant to developing a quality system and if a chart representing this does not already exist it may be worth drawing one as well. However, we recommend that the current departmental structure should not be the basis of the quality system since it is likely to change quicker than the basic processes. Also, it may be that if a similar process is carried out by several departments, it may be better to have a common set of procedures rather than one per department.

The type of chart shown in Figure 9.1 can be developed for any business since fundamentally all are strings of inputs (what goes into one of the boxes), processes (what happens within them) and outputs (what comes out, with the outputs from one process becoming the inputs of another). There is, however, the difficulty that some activities – mainly administrative ones such as accountancy, maintenance etc – do not fit into a process flow. Instead they provide the environment in which the whole operation works. It is usually enough, at this stage, to simply represent these as a detached 'support activities' box.

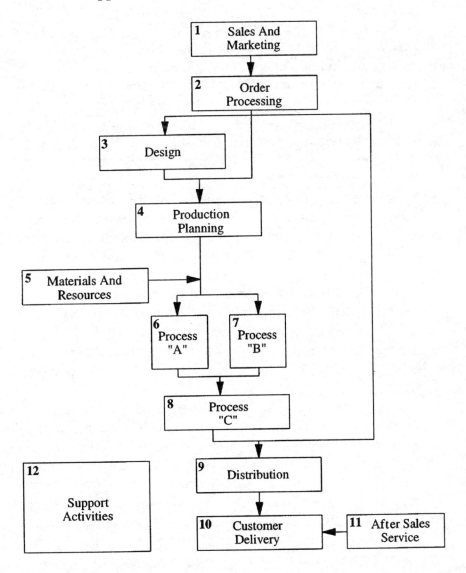

Figure 9.1   Example of process analysis

The main purpose of process analysis is to provide a framework for deciding what procedures are needed, their structure and ultimately their content. Such analysis may also lead to considering whether the current organisational structure is the best (this is basically the concept of 're-engineering' currently so in vogue). However, re-organising the company and putting in place a quality system may be too much to do at one time!

Process analysis also aids making a final decision on the scope of the quality system, including whether it should be applied to all the business or just part (there are problems with the latter approach – see Chapter 4) and which functions should fall within or outside the system. Some activities such as accountancy, much of personnel management, marketing except for any contract review element, and building maintenance are not covered in the requirements of the Standard and can be left outside the scope of a quality system. Possibly, however, it may be considered desirable to cover these as well to achieve the benefits of a more organised approach but the system will be that much more complicated and more likely to go wrong. Finally, process analysis may be the stage to make a firm decision on design. The extent to which the company is involved in design activities (bearing in mind the breadth of the concept in ISO 9000) should be clear from the analysis and a decision can be taken on whether the ISO 9001 or 9002 model of quality assurance should be applied.

At its simplest, process analysis is a matter of someone with an ability for clear thinking and who knows the business, sitting down with blank paper and developing a good visual model of the process. This may be done by the project manager or someone else. The very wide staff consultation process we recommend when it comes to writing procedures is not needed at this stage but obviously advice on how processes work should be sought and the finished chart should be discussed and agreed by the company's management team.

REVIEW

The review is carried out to relate the requirements of the Standard to the processes carried out in the company (represented in the process analysis chart) and current working practices. The end result of this stage is, therefore, some sort of list of what needs to be done to produce the quality system. The work of the review is generally best done by one person (the project manager or someone to whom he or she delegates the task) but who consults many others in the organisation to establish current practice (although not in the detail required in the next step – developing and drafting procedures). The end result of the review should also be considered by the management team as it will have important consequences in terms of the work required later and the structure of the final outcome.

An essential requirement for the review is a good understanding of the Standard and its requirements and this is why consultants can provide a very useful input at this stage. However, if a 'translation' document for the particular industry is available this may be a useful guide. Obviously, by now, a copy of the relevant ISO model (9001 or 9002 depending on the inclusion or otherwise of design) is also essential – in any case it will be required at the time of the assessment.

The review is best documented in a formal way. In the specimen extract below, the headings and summary contents of the Standard are set out on the left, whilst on the right is a description of the current situation. For the purposes of the review, the current practice description can fall into one of four categories:

1. No procedures or established methods exist. Almost certainly this will be the case in relation to the quality system control requirements such as corrective action and auditing. In these cases not only will procedures need drafting but new sorts of activities will have to be carried out to meet ISO 9000.

2. There are established working methods (which might be followed more or less consistently) but these are not documented in any way.

3. Some sort of documentation exists – operating manuals, memos, departmental instructions, record books and forms etc. In this case all that may be required is re-formatting the documents.

4. There appears to be no relevant application of the requirement.

The focus of the descriptions of current practice is, therefore, in relation to documented procedures (and linked records and forms) or the lack of them. The other type of documentation required for a quality system (eg the Quality Manual) needs only noting in passing at the review stage.

Specimen Extract From Review Report

Requirement	*Current Practice*
4.6 Purchasing	
4.6.1 General	There are well established purchasing methods but not set out in formal procedures.
4.6.2 Evaluation	
Selection	There are established suppliers and some management control over the use of new ones.
Evaluation	No systematic methods, though correspondence files are well kept and identify problems.
Methods of control	Visits are made by the production manager to key suppliers and he makes notes for his own purposes.
Supplier lists & records	None kept systematically.
4.6.3 Purchasing data	Written purchase orders/purchase number system in use.
4.6.4 Verification	There have as yet been no contracts requiring this (requirement has no practical application?).

All the headings of the Standard should be covered in the review and recorded in some form similar to the example shown above.

Once the review work is done (including discussing and agreeing it with colleagues) a list can be prepared of the procedures required (and other documentation such as the quality manual) and in each case with some indication of how much work is likely to be required to produce the document – obviously more work will be needed where there are no procedures at all and rather less if existing documentation merely needs re-formatting. Whilst the review follows the order of the Standard's headings, the list of required procedures is better linked to the process analysis chart and it is useful to decide on a provisional numbering system (in Figure 9.1 each box is numbered and these can be the numbers of procedure groups).

DEVELOPING AND DRAFTING PROCEDURES

The process analysis and review work can often be carried out within a week or so. Developing and drafting procedures is a different matter with the work often stretching over several months and representing most of the time needed for preparing the whole system. Partly this is because many people have to be drawn into the work. It is at this stage that staff involvement is so important and the programme has to be fitted around their day to day commitments.

The first step in preparing the procedures is for the project manager to decide who will have the primary responsibility for the task. In a small business it may be only one person, and often the project manager, who does this, but in larger organisations it will be necessary to have a number of procedure 'scribes'. Some training will be needed. This can be through external paid-for courses or be led by a consultant involved in the project. However, even where the concept of a quality system is very novel, internal do-it-youself training is quite feasible. There is also a need to agree and set formats for finished procedures; as we discussed in Chapter 8, it really does not matter what the format is as long as it is standard. A specimen procedure, to use as a model, is the best way of doing this. It is probably also useful to set limits to the length of procedure sets (the specimen corrective action procedures at the end of Chapter 8 is a set) since shorter ones are almost always better than longer ones. Where a process appears to need a procedure longer than this maximum all that is needed is to split it into two or more sets.

Once the team is trained and briefed, responsibilities and deadlines can be set by the project manager. There is of course no need to prepare procedures in the order of their final numbering if there is a good reason to do otherwise.

The method of preparing procedures should include practical means of involving the staff concerned and at least this should include a representative group of those working on a particular process (and not just the department manager or deputy). There are two reasons for this. Firstly only through this involvement will the staff feel that they 'own' the procedure and this is necessary for successful implementation. Secondly, often only the people involved in working a process know what happens in sufficient detail to develop a realistic procedure.

There are various techniques for achieving involvement, but the one we strongly recommend is charting. This approach initially represents a process pictorially and the big advantage is that all levels of staff will find it easy to think in this way. The process of developing procedures may (and generally should) involve staff who are not used to writing documents but with only limited prompting can start to think creatively and logically using the boxes and lines making up charts.

Charting is really an expansion of the output from the initial process analysis and involves showing all the sub-systems making up each major process 'box' (as in Figure 9.1). Figure 9.2 shows an example of such a chart which is, in this case, drawn from a professional service business – market research.

The chart is prepared by the procedure leader convening the relevant group of staff and asking them to tell him what happens, step by step, in the process. He or she then charts it, in rough,

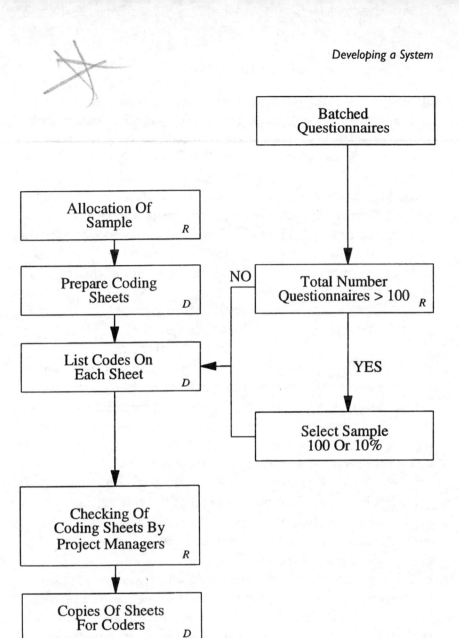

R = RECORD REQUIRED?
D = PROCESS DOCUMENT

Figure 9.2   Examples of charting

there and then (the chart in Figure 9.2 is of course an edited and tidied version of an original and would generally not be needed to this standard). Perhaps after an initially slow start, the group will soon grasp what is required and work happily with the pictorial representation of their process. The aim, at least initially, should be to show the process as it is actually carried out 'warts and all'. It is quite likely that once represented in this way, some steps in the process will appear inefficient or unnecessary and the decision will soon have to be made whether to base the procedure on what happens now rather on how the process could be better carried out. We cannot be categorical on this point, but do tend to the view that it is better to base procedures on current practice and then make changes for the better through the implemented system. This way will reduce the problems of implementation and may even make it easier to introduce effective changes (this is one of the benefits of a quality system). There is also a similar problem where different staff work in different ways or where some recognised good practice is followed 'when possible'. The leader's task in this case is to arrive at a reasonable common ground. For these and other reasons the chart will look very messy with crossing-outs and overwriting. But no matter. It is a working tool only and not an end in itself. If necessary, a fair copy can be drafted for when the procedure writing starts. Exceptionally it may be necessary to show this fair copy to the group to make sure it is correct.

The finished chart will represent more or less everything that happens in the process. However, as discussed in Chapter 8, a procedure should not be a comprehensive catalogue of every activity involved in a process but concentrate on the steps which are relevant to quality. The finished chart should, therefore, be reviewed to highlight these essential areas. In this case the leader may need to take a rather more active role but staff involvement is still needed. There is also the question of how any quality records which may be needed in the procedure are to be taken (in Figure 9.2 this is annotated). The leader (or others such as the project manager) also needs to consider whether activities required by the Standard are absent from the existing process – eg if no inspection or testing is carried out in a major process, a relevant requirement (*4.10 inspection and testing*) may not be met and a change in working practice will be neccesary to comply with ISO 9000. The review records will be very useful in making the necessary judgements. However, the need to change processes in this way will generally be the exception rather than the rule apart from in meeting the more procedural requirements such as those relating to system control.

This recommended approach may seem rather long-winded, but once the chart is finalised the major work is done. All that is then required is writing out the procedure in words – typically an hour's or so job. If desired, the chart can form part of the finished procedure or even make up most of it. This can be very effective, although a practical difficulty is often that drawing (and later revising) charts of a quality to include in a procedure manual is not as easy as wordsmithing. Once finalised, the draft should then be discussed with the group involved in its development and if necessary amended. A simple comprehension check among staff who will use the procedures is also a good idea. Finally, the draft should be formally approved and authorised – by the project manager, the whole management team, the chief executive or whatever approach is decided to be appropriate.

In a few areas such as those concerned with quality system control, the chart-to-procedure method will prove to be less effective. This is because in these cases there is no existing process to chart. Also the need for staff involvement is rather less; most staff will have only a limited need to use the final procedure. In these cases it may be better to develop the procedure directly from the requirements of the standard but taking into account the unique culture of the organisation. A consultant can often usefully and efficiently work on this part of the procedure.

Once the required procedures have been drafted and approved, all that remains to produce the procedure manual is to print the required number of controlled copies (if desired, on special paper etc), put them together in a binder and include front-end document and circulation lists. The forms which are an integral part of the system and meet the requirement for quality records should have been prepared as part of procedure drafting. The Standard has no requirement for a high quality of documentation although we believe that some effort in this respect is needed. Well presented documents just seem more appropriate for a quality system and there is no harm in impressing assessors or others who may see the quality manuals etc. Also care in this respect makes a statement to staff about the company's commitment to quality.

OTHER DOCUMENTATION

Apart from the procedures, there are other documents making up a whole quality system: particularly the quality policy and quality manual. Both documents need drafting, approving and the controlled copies printed. Some purists argue that the quality policy, if not the quality manual, should be prepared at the start rather than at the end of the whole process. The argument in the case of the policy is that this expresses the commitment to the whole project and ought to be made and communicated at the start. However, the policy can be understood and the commitment recognised before it is formally drafted and a benefit of doing this later is that, with a greater understanding of quality systems and ISO 9000, the document will be better worded. This applies even more so in the case of the quality manual and indeed if, as we recommended, this document is thoroughly cross-referenced to the procedures, it cannot be finalised until all these are complete.

10

Implementation

With all the quality system documentation written and printed, the emphasis switches to implementation. Getting the system to work. Various aspects of this, including the vital activity of auditing, are discussed in this chapter.

DOCUMENTATION AND OTHER RESOURCES

Chapter 9 took the project to where all the manuals and other documents are ready for use. All that remains to do now is to make sure that they are available throughout the company. All staff must have easy access to the procedures or at least those relevant to their day to day work. However, one copy per person is not recommended; document control is likely to become very difficult, if not impossible. One copy per area or department is more sensible. Copies of all forms and similar record material, as specified in the procedures, also need to be ready for use, in sufficient volume and by now the filing arrangements for the completed records should have been thought through and put in place.

Because its day to day use is limited, the quality manual does not have to be as widely distributed as the procedures but often it is as easy as not to have it in the same binder. Otherwise, controlled copies of the quality manual can be held at a central point provided they are available to staff. The quality policy is, however, another matter and this must be effectively communicated. Copies displayed around the premises are as convenient a way of achieving this as any.

Apart from the documentation and associated filing, the only other physical resources which may need to be made ready are inspection, testing and measuring equipment. In most cases the quality system will have not brought in any new equipment of this sort, but the relevant procedures may require changes to be made in how they are kept and used.

TRAINING FOR THE QUALITY SYSTEM

Before start-up of the system, staff will require training in how to use it and carry out some new tasks. The latter include those carried out by staff with specialised roles in the system and especially that of management representative (however titled) and internal auditors. The work of auditing is considered shortly and we will leave until then the training required by those carrying out this important work. The management representative is also pivotal to the success of the system and he or she needs to understand what is required in this role, which, except in large organisations, is likely to be a part-time responsibility. Where, as is quite common, the project leader takes over as management representative there is not likely to be any need for formal training since he or she should have the necessary understanding through overseeing the creation of the whole system. Where someone else takes on the role, a thorough briefing by the project leader is probably sufficient initial training. In either case, it is useful for the management representative to draw up a checklist of all the tasks required. Most of these should be spelt out in relevant procedures, especially those relating to quality system control. The management representative is also often the head of the audit team and needs to be as well trained in this area as the auditors.

The only other specialised roles in running a quality system relate to inspection and testing activities. Those involved in this work need to be adequately trained in the work. However, it is quite likely that the quality system has introduced few, if any, new methods in this respect and specialised training may be scarcely needed.

As well as the specialists, all staff will need to understand what the new quality system requires of them. First and foremost this means the procedures affecting their day to day work, and the number that apply will often be related to seniority. For someone working just one machine for example, a very few procedures may be all that need concern him, at least for most of the time. A department manager, however, needs to be familiar with all the procedures covering the department and the production manager will have to come to terms with nearly all the system. However, if as we recommended, staff were very much involved in developing 'their' procedures, the training required in this respect should be minimal. Furthermore, well drafted procedures should be self-explanatory and need the minimum of additional explanation.

As well as training in the procedures which immediately affect them, staff need an overview of the whole system and of some key underlying principles. In this respect, system induction is as much about motivation as training. Some suggested topics to cover are listed below.

Quality System Induction Topics

Benefits. Why a quality system to ISO 9000 is to be implemented and why the company and its staff will benefit (see Chapter 3).

The parts of the system. The quality policy and manual. The procedures and where to access them. The need to consult procedures. Forms and other records.

Controlled documentation. Identifying controlled documents. What control means and its importance. Controlled documents not to be changed except through a specific procedure. Uncontrolled copies of procedures are not to be used.

Procedures are mandatory. Procedures are whatever they are in the current controlled manual. They must be followed, by all staff, wherever they apply and even where they appear not to work well or at all.

System change. The system can be changed and it is to be expected that some initial procedures will prove to be deficient. There are procedures controlling change.

Solving problems. The quality system is a tool for making improvements. Problems include those arising in the work as well as in the operation of the quality system. Participation in problem solving through the corrective action procedure. Raising and investigating corrective actions. Corrective actions are not a 'blaming' device.

Auditing. Why it is required. Who will do auditing. What they will do. Auditors identify problems – not solve them or apportion blame.

Assessment. The timetable. What is involved.

Effective methods of induction will vary considerably between different types of organisations and little can be usefully said that is of general application. However, the induction training should be used to communicate and reinforce the commitment of senior management to the system – the chief executive should be involved.

START-UP

After training is complete the system needs to be started up as soon as possible. There are two alternative approaches; big bang and roll-out. In the former case, a 'Q-day' is set and on that day (with a few speeches made and the band playing) everyone, throughout the company, starts working to the procedures. The advantage is that it is clear when the system starts and nobody should have any doubts about this. The excitement of Q-day is also a strong motivator. The major problem may be short term disruption as the system settles down. The alternative roll-out approach is to start operating procedures department by department and probably with training staggered accordingly. This lessens any overall disruption and also provides an element of piloting (procedures can be implemented as soon as they are authorised). The disadvantages include a loss of impact and consequent motivation; implementation by stealth may become a damp squib. Also there may be practical problems in following only part of a system – procedures may require something to have been done up-stream by departments which have not yet implemented the quality system. A judgement and choice between big bang and roll-out needs to be made.

A similar issue relates to work in progress. On start-up of the system, are the procedures to be applied to work on all products or projects from then on or only on products or projects entering the overall process at that time? There can be problems in either approach but the key factor is the length of the production cycle. Where it is short, the system can be followed as products enter the process and it may be that apart from any stock, there are no products part way through production on Q-day morning. If, however, the business involves long-term projects lasting weeks or months (eg capital plant) it will be better to apply the system from the point each project has reached on start-up day. This may involve some problems where up-stream procedures have not been applied, but the alternative would be to delay full implementation for far too long.

AUDITING

The importance of internal auditing cannot be over-emphasised. It is a requirement of the Standard but even if it was not it would be essential. A quality system which is not audited will not work and will quickly fade away. On the other hand, if the system is reasonably well thought out, effective auditing and the actions taken as the result of audits will virtually guarantee success at assessment. Indeed, if at the assessment, major problems (of which the company's management were unaware) are identified, the auditing has not been adequate. Internal auditing, therefore, mirrors the assessment (or vice versa).

In this section we describe the process and work of auditing and then discuss the selection and training of auditors. At the end of the chapter, specimen procedures for internal auditing are provided; these will hopefully assist readers in understanding the process and may be a model to adapt.

The overall objective of internal auditing is to establish whether the quality system is effective and is being followed. The converse of this is that any problems arising from the quality system, including non-conformity with the specified procedures, will be identified and can then be addressed (through corrective and preventive action – see below). However, it is worth making the point that the emphasis is on the positive – establishing the system works – rather than finding faults. This is also true of assessors.

A planned approach to auditing is required so that all parts of the system and processes are covered over a period – usually a year, although the initial aim should be to cover the whole system at least once between implementation and assessment and this period may only be three or four months. Planning should also take into account how critical processes are for quality and consider on this basis the need for more frequent auditing in some areas rather than others. Similarly, after a period, the results of initial audits may indicate where greater attention is needed – eg where staff have had problems following procedures. Lastly, planning needs to allow some flexibility so that urgent problems can be addressed – serious quality defects may indicate that the operation of the quality system in one area needs auditing imme- diately. Taking these and other factors into account, an audit schedule should be prepared on implementation and thereafter every year. This work is generally carried out by the management representative whose responsibilities often include managing the audit process and ensuring that scheduled audits take place.

Each audit needs a defined scope in relation to the processes of the business (eg the operation of the quality system in preparing meals for passengers), or departments (eg customer account handling) or specific procedures (eg those relating to purchas- ing); in many cases all three will amount to one and the same. Auditors from the trained team (this may number only one or two in a small business) are then assigned to the work and dates agreed for completion. As well as the schedule, each audit should be planned and in this case it is a matter of auditors (perhaps in conjunction with the management representative) preparing a written checklist of what specifically they are going to examine during the audit. This is likely to include procedure references and a summary of the activities required by these procedures. The procedures included on the checklist (and, therefore, audited) may well be just a sample of all those applying in the area. Under each such heading, the sort of evidence sought in the audit (see shortly) can also be listed. In preparing a checklist, the auditor must of course have available a controlled copy of the procedures and, after the system has been in place for some time, records of previous audits of the area or relevant corrective actions need to be considered. Apart from the checklist, preparation should also include making arrangements with the staff working in the area to be audited – there is no point turning up and finding everyone away.

The actual work of the audit involves establishing whether the selected procedures are being followed in practice. It is essential that this is determined *in detail*; it is not enough that the staff in the department are generally well disposed to the system or 'more or less' follow it. The question in the case of each procedure or part of a procedure examined is whether the actions are in conformity to that which is specified. If the procedures require an operator to spin a plate on top of a walking stick whilst operating the control button, then this is what *should* be done (one outcome of the audit might be that such a silly procedure is changed!). For this reason, one quality required of an auditor is an ability to get down to detail. There are four general methods the auditor can use to test whether procedures are being followed and those which are to be used should be considered in advance and included in the checklist.

FOUR METHODS OF TESTING PROCEDURE IMPLEMENTATION

1. Observation
2. Questioning
3. Records provided
4. Records selected

Firstly the auditor can observe staff to see whether their work matches up to the procedures. Obviously a limitation here is that staff may work in a different way when being observed. Secondly auditors can talk to staff (questioning) and check whether they know what they ought to be doing; if they do not, how can they be following the procedures? DHL International puts some emphasis on this approach. Thirdly auditors can ask staff to show them the records (records provided) made in following a procedure – forms completed, log books filled, computer data entered etc. Finally the auditors can themselves select relevant records (records selected) and this ought to be possible if the filing system is adequate. This makes sure that the staff being audited do not just show the records of cases where they have followed the procedures. In any audit, all four methods can be used but where possible, most of the evidence should be 'hard' – records made in compliance with the system.

Using these approaches, an auditor may identify a problem; incomplete records, entries missed, inadequate filing etc – evidence that a procedure is not being implemented. The auditor should record this as an audit finding with adequate details (eg the relevant procedure, the job number where the case was found etc) and ideally get the staff involved to agree that the deficiency exists. This should not be difficult – eg either the form has been filled in or it has not. Having done this, the job of the auditor is complete and it is essential to understand that the auditors role does not extend to establishing *why* the problem has arisen and still less blaming anybody for not following the system. Possibly the procedure has not been followed because staff do not understand what is required, or wilfully ignore the procedure. Alternatively the problem may lie in the procedure – perhaps it cannot be followed. However, these are not issues for the auditor (if staff give reasons for non-compliance, these can be noted of course but the auditor should be neutral on whether or not such reasons are good and valid). Also, it is not an auditor's job to find a solution to the problem; this, as well as an investigation of the causes, is addressed outside the audit process itself (by corrective and preventive action – see below).

On completion of the audit, a written report should be made and discussed with the management representative (or whoever heads up auditing). The report should also be given to and discussed with the staff audited. Where a problem has been identified in the audit, the management representative must decide what needs to be done about it and this normally leads into the corrective action procedure, to be discussed shortly. Where a corrective action is raised as a result of an audit, follow-up is required. This involves auditors examining the specific area where the problem was found (eg non-compliance with one procedure) and establishing whether the problem has been solved. Such follow-ups need to be carried out within a defined period but one which allows time for the corrective action process to have been completed – in the specimen procedure the time limit is 45 days. Where the follow-up audit identifies that the problem is still not solved, an effective system requires something further to be done until the problem is solved (in the specimen procedure, the corrective action – follow-up audit loop, is potentially followed until the problem is finally dealt with). Both the original audits and follow-ups should be adequately recorded and filed – again see the specimen procedure.

In selecting staff to carry out internal auditing, the first consideration is independence. No one can audit themselves or the area where they normally work. The two ways of achieving this are to use staff who are not involved in any of the processes covered by the quality system – eg from the accounts department or freelances brought in from outside – or through cross-auditing. In the latter approach, staff in an number of areas are trained as auditors and perform this role outside their own area – Datac Adhesives have used this method successfully. In either case, a decision on the number of auditors to train needs to be made and relevant considerations include the size of the business, the number of procedures in the system and the need to be able to cover for the absence of some auditors. There may be an argument for having too many rather than too few but there can be problems if each auditor's work is carried out too infrequently to acquire good experience.

Auditors also need some personal qualities. These include the attention to detail already mentioned, human relations skills and the strength to stand by their own judgement. Possibly an auditor may be browbeaten by a senior manager who is concerned not to have some problem identified. In such cases the auditor must stick by their findings and not accept three fingers are there when they can only see two. Auditors also need to be able to prepare simple but easily understood reports of their findings.

Except in the largest of companies, auditing will be a part-time role combined with some mainstream duties and possibly including other specific quality tasks – DHL International's auditors are also quality representatives involved in the company's overall TQM programme. Such combination of roles is inevitable and quite acceptable. However, the staff involved must learn to recognise when they are wearing their auditing hat and not attempt to extend the audit process to either finding the cause of problems or their solution. This sort of detachment needs to be learnt and discussed as part of training for the work.

In a small company, adequate auditor training can often be in-house with the management representative and the auditors learning together what the process entails. This should be on-going with frequent meetings held to discuss how well the audit work is going. Initially, such meetings should follow every audit. Formal training by outsiders can also be considered. These can be led by the consultant involved with the whole project (if there is one) or by booking onto one of the many courses on offer in this area. These range from one day sessions, through the two day Registered Internal Auditor[1] qualification (appropriate for ISO 9000 systems) up to much longer courses to become a lead assessor (which is way beyond what is neccesary in a small business).

Our final advice on auditing is to get on with it as soon as possible. Within a week or two of start-up, carry out a first audit and then keep it up so that the whole system has been covered by the time of assessment. This means that auditors need to be selected and initially trained by Q-day.

CORRECTIVE ACTION

Corrective action (we shall use this term to cover both corrective and preventive action as per heading *4.14* of the Standard) is the quality system process followed to deal with a problem identified through internal audits. However, the same process is also followed to deal with problems identified in other ways including customer complaints, product faults, breakdowns of the process and where a member of staff simply has a good idea for changing the quality system (which implies some deficiency in the existing arrangements). Put positively, corrective action is, therefore, a mechanism for *quality improvement* and there is everything to gain from encouraging all staff to be involved and raise corrective actions. However, a word of warning. Despite its severe sounding name, corrective action should not be used as a method of punishing or disciplining staff. In some companies, the phrase 'raising a corrective action against so and so' is used. This is a misuse of a quality system. True, occasionally, wilful disregard of the quality system may need to be dealt with by management but this should be seen as a last resort and not an intrinsic part of the quality assurance approach.

---

[1] To the standard of the International Registry of Certificated Assessors which is maintained in the UK by the IQA (see Chapter 9 for contact details).

The corrective action process is normally administered by the management representative and closely links into leadership of the auditing process. A documented procedure is required and the key elements of it will include:

○ Initiation of the process, eg by a member of staff (including an auditor) requesting a corrective action report form and writing a statement of the problem. The management representative can be given some discretion to weed out frivolous or inappropriate requests.

○ An investigator is selected by the management representative and asked to consider the causes of the problem and a possible solution.

○ The investigator, having decided the causes of the problems and considered a solution, then makes a report to the management representative.

Obviously the investigator is the key to the effective use of the process and his or her selection is a matter for the management representative's good judgement. Generally, what is required is some knowledge and expertise in the area where the problem exists and often the immediate manager is an obvious choice. However, sometimes it may be better to bring in an outsider to look at the problem with fresh eyes.

Where it appears obvious that the problem is simply one of a member of staff not following a procedure, the management representative can consider giving that person the job of investigating the cause and proposing a solution. They will then have to recognise that they should be following the system. However, it also gives them the opportunity to explain why the procedure is difficult to follow; possibly compliance is just not practical. Such an approach can be useful but there is a danger that it will turn the corrective action process into a disciplining device – staff are punished by being given the chore of an investigation.

The person raising the corrective action (identifying the problem) should not normally be appointed as the investigator and this is definitely the case for auditors. One exception, however, is where the procedure is used to consider a suggested improvement. In this case the initiation, investigation and recommendation are, in practice, all one.

The investigation process may take hardly any time at all where the cause and solution of the problem are transparent. In other cases the investigation may be spread over several weeks, involve a detailed examination of relevant records and wide consultation among staff affected. Whatever is involved, however, the final recommendation can take two basic forms; a change to the system or a change to the system's implementation when the problems lie not in the procedures but in staff following them (or not). In the early days of operating the system, both sorts of problems are likely to be found but particularly the latter which may need addressing through additional training. However, often the problem is just that a member of staff does not understand a procedure and the investigation effectively solves the matter – the person concerned learns what is required.

Whatever recommendation is made, the company's management must then decide whether to implement it. Where this involves a substantial change to the quality system this decision ought to be made in a management review meeting (see shortly) but in other cases, and especially where all that is needed is simple re-training, it will usually be more appropriate for the management representative to take the action (the exercise of such discretion can be in the procedures).

Where, as a result of corrective action, a decision is made to change the quality system this should be done through an appropriate procedure to ensure the quality system documentation remains under control (see comments on this in Chapter 8) and conversely it is good practice to only allow changes to the system through the corrective action procedure. It is impractical to change the system too often (for one thing there is quite a lot of work involved in amending all the controlled copies) and, therefore, a specific change may be delayed until a number can be dealt with together. However, there should be no reluctance to change the system if this is necessary and particularly in the initial period of its operation. Inevitably, and no matter how much thought has gone into its creation, the bedding-in period will require the initial version of some procedures (and associated forms) to be amended.

MANAGEMENT REVIEW

A management review is simply the occasion when the senior management of a company considers how well or otherwise the quality system is working and makes decisions about its future. Whatever form they take, it is essential that these meetings are held in the bedding-in period after implementation; they should happen then more rather than less frequently. The management representative has a key role in the meeting including making formal reports on the findings of audits, the outcomes of corrective action and any changes made to the system since the last meeting. Other matters that need to be specifically discussed are any customer complaints (or for that matter positive feedback) and any problems in the process (perhaps with departmental managers making reports). Where corrective action decisions are referred to the management review meeting, the report from the investigator should be considered, a decision made and responsibilities for action agreed.

Although the Standard does not require management review to be covered by a procedure, a short one – a page or so – is in practice advisable. The essential issues to cover include:

O Who is to attend the meetings, notice of meetings and what constitutes a quorum.

O The frequency of the meetings – quarterly is probably the normal minimum but in the bedding-in period they need to be monthly (this need not be written into the procedures).

O An agenda – this can be a standard format for every meeting.

O Recording arrangements – formal minutes are appropriate and someone needs to take them (usually the management representative).

Management review meetings are the third corner of the quality triangle illustrated at the end of Chapter 7 and taken together with internal audits and corrective action, provide a powerful mechanism for successfully implementing a quality system. Moreover, the mechanisms of the triangle help ensure that the full benefits of quality assurance are obtained, including progressive quality improvement.

Specimen Document

PROCEDURE 11.3
INTERNAL QUALITY AUDITS

Purpose
To define procedures to ensure that the Quality System and all areas and processes covered by the System are adequately audited.

Scope
All parts of the Quality System and areas and processes covered by the System.

References
Procedure Manual – 11.4

Definitions
IQA – staff carrying out internal quality audits.

Documentation
11.3.3/1 Register Of Audits
11.3.4/1 Audit Report Form
11.3.5/1 Follow-up Audit Report

11.3 V2 1/1/95 QM 1/4

Procedures

11.3.1 *Internal Quality Audit Team*

The Quality Manager shall appoint staff to act as Internal Quality Auditors (IQA) and record their names and date of appointment.

The Quality Manager may act as an IQA.

The Quality Manager shall ensure IQA are adequately trained and shall prepare and file records of this training.

11.3.2 *Frequency And Coverage Of Audits*

At least one audit shall be carried out in each quarter of the year.

Over a year all parts of the Quality system shall be audited at least once.

In January of each year the Quality Manager shall prepare a schedule of audits for the whole year.

11.3.3 *IQA Meetings*

The Quality Manager shall from time to time convene meetings of IQA to:

Assign audits to the audit team or individual auditors, by reference to specific elements of the Quality System. The audits shall be numbered sequentially with the relevant details recorded in the Register Of Audits – 11.3.3/1

and as the Quality Manager considers appropriate to:

Review the progress of audit work during the current year.

Assess IQA performance and review training needs.

11.3.4 *Audit Work*

On receipt of an audit assignment, the IQA shall review the records of any relevant previous audits carried out within the preceding two years and consider any implications of these for the planned audit.

11.3 V2 1/1/95 QM 2/4

An appropriate audit checklist shall be prepared by the IQA in advance of each audit.

The IQA shall arrange convenient times for the audit with staff involved in the working areas to be covered in the audit.

The IQA shall then carry out the audit and discuss the results with the Quality Manager and the staff covered by the audit.

Where appropriate the Quality Manager shall issue Corrective Action Forms – see 11.4.

The IQA shall then prepare a report of the audit using the form 11.3.4/1 and give this to the Quality Manager along with any appropriately completed Corrective Action Forms raised as a result of the audit.

The Quality Manager shall make relevant entries in the Register of Audits 11.3.3/1, file the audit report and where appropriate follow the Corrective Action Procedure – see 11.4.

11.3.5 *Follow-up Audits*

If a Corrective Action is raised as a result of an audit, the Quality Manager shall assign the IQA to carry out a follow-up audit within 45 days of the date of the original audit.

The purpose of such follow-up audits shall be to establish the results achieved by each Corrective Action raised as a result of the original audit.

On completion of a follow-up audit, the IQA shall prepare a Follow Up Audit Report – 11.3.5/1 and pass this to the Quality Manager who shall make appropriate entries in the Register Of Audits 11.3.3/1 and file the report.

If the Quality Manager considers that the results of a follow-up audit are unsatisfactory a further Corrective Action will be issued, the Corrective Action Procedure – see 11.4 – followed and a further follow-up audit assigned as per above.

11.3 V2 1/1/95 QM 3/4

11.3.6 Retention Of Records

The Quality Manager shall be responsible for keeping all records relating to Procedures 11.3 and retain them for a minimum period of five years after which they may be destroyed.

11.3 V2 1/1/95 QM 4/4

11.3.3/1   **Register Of Audits**   V1

Audit No	Date Started	Audit Coverage	Auditor	Date Report Received	Date Follow-up Audit

11.3.4/1   **Audit Report**   **V1**

Audit No.		Date of Audit		Date of Report	
Audit Coverage		Job Nos	Administrative Procedures		

Findings - As per Corrective Action Form Numbers:

Observations:

Recommendations:

Signature (Auditor)

11.3.5/1   Follow-up Audit Report   VI

Audit No:		Date of Audit:		Date of Report:	
Corrective Action Form No.		Complete		Not Complete	

Notes:

Signature (Auditor)

11

Assessment

Whatever long term benefits are sought from ISO 9000, the immediate goal is nearly always successful assessment and gaining the certificate. Selecting assessors, preparing for assessment and what the latter entails are the subjects of this chapter.

SELECTING ASSESSORS

Anyone can set up in business and award ISO 9000 certificates. However, how much credence ISO 9000 carries if assessed by an unrecognised and unregistered concern is another matter. The authoritative UK guide to who has ISO 9000 is a list published and updated by the Dti. Inclusion on this depends on certification by a UKAS[1] accredited assessor body. Any company serious about ISO 9000 therefore needs to be assessed by such approved assessors.

Not that there is any shortage of accredited assessors to choose from – about thirty currently exist and the number continues to grow. UKAS will send an up to date list on request. These bodies fall into two broad groups – specialists and generalists. The former assess in only a narrow industry field – eg National Approval Council for Security Systems – and obviously can only be considered by businesses in that field. The generalists will assess any or at least most businesses and examples of these include BSI QA, Bureau Veritas, Det Norske Veritas, Lloyds Register, NQA and SGS Yarsley. However, whether or not they

---

[1] UKAS (United Kingdom Accreditation Service) – 13 Palace Street, London, SW1E 5HS. Tel. 0171-233 7111.

specialise, each body assesses ISO 9000 in the same way (and is in turn assessed by UKAS) and their certificates are of equal worth.

The first step in selecting an assessor is to draw up an initial list of potential bodies, contact each one, briefly describe your assessment requirements and provide a short description of your own business. It is important to establish, at this stage, whether the organisation includes your particular industry in their 'scope of accreditation'. Assessment bodies do not have blanket approval from UKAS but are accredited for specific types of business. To be included on the Dti list a company must be assessed by a body with an appropriate scope. Wherever possible,[2] therefore, only such organisations are worth considering as assessors.

From the initial response, a shortlist can be drawn up and quotations requested. Most assessment bodies will make a preliminary visit before preparing a quotation and proposal and this also gives the client company an opportunity to make some judgement on the service they are likely to receive. As discussed shortly, assessment is not just a once off process and the quotations provided are usually for a three year cycle of assessment and surveillance. For a one-site business employing 40 people, this package is likely to cost in the order of £2000 pa but individual assessor bodies vary quite widely in their pricing and if only for this reason, competitive quotations are advised. Some assessors have special budget schemes for very small businesses and these may be well worth considering.

Apart from in their charging, another variation between assessors is in the lead times from acceptance of their proposal to assessment, and this may be a determining factor in the choice made. However, as discussed shortly, all quality systems need bedding-in for several months before assessment and if the selection process is started at around the time of implementation,

---

[2]   A few specialised businesses may find a problem if no assessment body is as yet accredited for the activity. Some bodies (eg SGS Yarsley) undertake to seek accreditation for all businesses they assess.

virtually all the bodies are likely to meet a realistic timetable. Beyond costs and timing, choice is a matter of judging how well you will be able to work with the assessor body for the next three or more years. The views of other companies in your own industry, who have already been assessed, may be worth having.

PREPARING FOR ASSESSMENT

A quality system cannot be realistically assessed until it has operated for some time. Effective implementation takes some bedding-in. Also, the assessment process involves the 'hard' evidence of completed records required by the procedures (although assessment, like internal auditing, can also include observing and talking to staff). Obviously, to build up an adequate body of such data takes time and until this is sufficient, a meaningful assessment cannot be carried out. For this reason, an assessment body will insist on an adequate bedding-in period.

How long is adequate for bedding-in? Most assessors are likely to require a minimum of about three months, but longer may well be more appropriate, depending on many aspects of a company, its organisation and its processes – a long production cycle for example, may need more bedding-in than a shorter one since longer is needed to build up experience of operating the complete system. There are arguments against being over-cautious and waiting too long for assessment but equally success at initial assessment is less likely if the pace is forced. DHL International recognised after a first incomplete assessment that they had rushed the bedding-in period and not identified and dealt with some of the teething problems.

As we discussed in Chapter 10, internal auditing is especially vital in the bedding-in period and the aim should be to have covered the whole system between implementation and assessment. In this way, problems should be identified and dealt with before an assessor picks them up. To labour the point; the importance of effective internal auditing cannot be over-emphasised.

An option before full assessment is a full pre-assessment audit. This is in effect a dummy run of the real thing and unlike routine internal audits is carried out by outsiders. A consultant involved throughout the project can be considered for this work although if the same individual is involved a certain independence is lacking. There are also many freelances and other independent organisations offering this service but the obvious choice for pre-assessment is the body who will carry out the final assessment. If nothing else you learn how the particular body handles the assessment process (although they all work to a standard there are some variations in their detailed approach).

Pre-assessment is probably particularly appropriate for companies developing a quality system with little or no outside help and, in such cases, it may identify areas of the system which are weak, or through misinterpretation, do not fully match up to ISO 9000. P&O European Ferries, for example, found that pre-assessment enabled them to bring a number of areas into line before final assessment. The only real argument against this type of check is its cost.

If an assessment body is used, their charges for pre-assessment are likely to be close to those made for the assessment itself. Arguably, therefore, a company concerned to keep costs down might as well trust to its own judgement on the effectiveness of its system and go straight to the real thing. If the first attempt is unsuccessful, then little is lost since the money saved on pre-assessment will cover a second full assessment. Against this view is the de-motivation for staff of 'failing' at the assessment. Also a pre-assessment may have a larger diagnostic element than a full assessment, where how to put right a problem is perhaps not fully discussed. Finally, another argument against spending money on pre-assessment is that it may be better to invest in more training for internal auditors who will then be able to carry out their own equivalent of a pre-assessment. Furthermore, the benefits are long term.

THE ASSESSMENT PROCESS

Once a contract with the chosen body is signed, the details of the process will be agreed with the management representative (one of his or her primary roles is liaison with the assessors) including the timetable and a date for the assessment visit. However, the on-site assessment is the second stage of the process and in the intervening period, a desk investigation is carried out. Assessors vary in the details of their desk investigation – some do it off-site and others make a special visit – but the objective is always restricted to establishing whether the documented quality system (controlled copies are examined) meets the requirements of the Standard. For example, do the purchasing procedures cover all that is required in heading 4.6? Whether or not the procedures are being followed is another matter and left aside until the later, on-site assessment.

As a result of the desk investigation, the assessor may very well raise a number of queries and these must be dealt with. However, these issues may just require clarification (and possibly arguing a case – it is not all black or white) rather than imply really serious deficiencies in the system. Discussions with the assessor should resolve what is required and a significant number of comments at this stage should not be a cause for despondency – Benfell Communications, for example, were faxed with several pages of queries as a result of the desk investigation but little was major or could not be easily dealt with. If, however, the assessors consider that the quality system has some major gaps in relation to ISO 9000 there is no point to an assessment visit until these are put right.

The on-site assessment process is in principle the same as internal audit work (assuming this is done properly) except that the whole system is covered at one go. How long this takes will depend on the manpower allocated by the assessors and the size and complexity of the organisation being assessed. The one-site firm with 40 employees, mentioned earlier, might for example, be allocated one assessor for two days. The assessment will involve systematically testing whether each element of the system is being implemented effectively and the procedures followed. The methods used for testing will be much as described for auditing (see Chapter 10) with an emphasis on 'hard' data but also with some questioning of staff (possibly including to test awareness of the quality policy). The first areas examined will nearly always be the records of internal auditing, corrective action and management review, including to check on any changes made since (or as result of) the desk investigation.

Most companies and their staff are likely to find assessment an ordeal however well prepared they are. The large majority of assessments are successful first time and bear in mind that the assessment body's outlook is positive – they want to find the evidence to award ISO 9000, although obvious problems in operating the system – non-conformities – cannot be just ignored. Non-conformities raised in an assessment are of two kinds; minor and major. Minor non-conformities are some defect in detail of operating the system. Some record forms, for example, are incomplete although the majority are correct. Benfell Communications, at their assessment, took rather too long to retrieve a product manual from the several thousand kept. Where such non-conformities are identified, the company is expected to put the matter right within a reasonable time (using their corrective action procedure) but the assessor will not make a special return visit to check this – in other words ISO 9000 will be awarded despite some minor non-conformities being found.

Major non-conformities are a different matter. These are raised if the assessor considers that a whole area of the quality system is not being implemented effectively – DHL International for example, were found on the first assessment visit to be having problems in exercising adequate document control (this is a common reason for non-conformities). Also, a number of minor non-conformities may be considered to add up to a major one, particularly if a consistent theme to them is apparent – eg poor record filing in most areas. The consequence of a major non-conformity is that ISO 9000 cannot be awarded until a further re-assessment visit (at extra cost) has been made. Obviously, if this happens, there is bound to be some disappointment but it would be wrong to dwell on this as failure. The problems identified should be addressed and solved and the assessment process can then be successfully completed.

SURVEILLANCE VISITS AND RE-ASSESSMENT

If all goes well at the assessment visit, the company will be given ISO 9000. You will probably be told so at the end of the visit but there is often a few weeks' delay until the certificate arrives and it is all official. The first thing to do is of course celebrate – by all means open a few bottles and when the certificate arrives make this an occasion. However, that is not the end of assessment. Every six months or so there is a follow-up surveillance visit to check that the quality system is still working and continues to meet ISO 9000. The approach is in principle the same as the initial assessment, although, because less time is taken (eg one man-day), only part of the whole system will be covered. A review of internal audit, corrective action and management review is usually the starting point of all such visits. As in the full assessment, minor or even major non-conformities can be raised and the first surveillance visit is likely to focus on whether any minor non-conformities raised at the assessment have been dealt with adequately. The consequence of a major non-conformity would be removal of ISO 9000 certification, although in practice this is unlikely without some warning given on a previous surveillance visit.

Individual assessment bodies vary in their practice on re-assessment. Some work to a three year cycle with a full assessment repeated after this period (and a new contract agreed). The argument for this policy is that after three years it is likely that the circumstances of the company will have changed so much that only a full re-assessment is appropriate. There is also the need to take account of any revisions to the Standard itself (eg as in 1994) although the requirement for a system to be changed for this reason is also covered in surveillance visits. However, most assessor bodies do not require full re-assessment and consider that instead continuous surveillance is adequate. The policy in this respect should be considered in evaluating assessors' quotations – over three years assessor A may be cheaper than B, but over five years more expensive if B does not require full re-assessment.

MARKETING ISO 9000

Finally, market ISO 9000. The marketing benefits of having ISO 9000 may not have been the primary objective but there is nearly always something to be gained. This, however, requires that you tell customers, potential customers, suppliers and others in your industry of your success and what this means to them. We do not mean much more than this in urging positive marketing of ISO 9000.

Simply telling the world of your success in gaining ISO 9000 is worthwhile but it is better still to build this into a complete message – particularly one that emphasises the benefits offered to customers. ISO 9000 can be too inward looking and there is a strong case for relating it all to a new ability to better meet customer needs. After all, this is the essence of the quality component so essential for the long term survival of any business. The changes brought into the business through ISO 9000, such as more rigorous reviews, extra inspection and testing, better planning and mechanisms for solving problems can all be featured as real quality benefits for customers.

One important marketing tool is the ISO 9000 certification logo which the assessor body allows its clients to use. This authoritatively differentiates a company which really has the Standard from those (too many) who make doubtful claims such as 'working towards ISO 9000', 'recognising ISO 9000' or 'a quality system to ISO 9000' – claims that may be without any real foundation. The logo is unique to each assessment body and there are rules governing its use and misuse. Broadly, it can be included on all sorts of publicity material (eg letterheads, quotations, adverts, vehicle livery etc) providing that no claim is made that a product meets the Standard – ISO 9000 is a standard for a company and its quality system and not for a specific product.

Methods of marketing ISO 9000 are all those available and appropriate to a specific business for any of its promotion aims. Gaining ISO 9000 should be newsworthy enough to at least get a free mention in the trade and perhaps local press. The ceremony of handing over the certificate is a bit trite but can still be the vehicle for a press release. Mailshots (eg perhaps of a professionally printed copy of the quality policy) and media advertising are also methods of communicating the achievement. The standing of ISO 9000 certification can also continue to be featured in the longer term advertising strategy. Nor should the salesforce's role be forgotten, even though much of their work is outside the scope of the Standard. They should be adequately briefed, trained to tell the ISO 9000 story and communicate customer benefits. Datac Adhesive's team carry a copy of the certificate with them at all times.

12

Beyond ISO 9000

Some organisations, especially those which were in some way forced into ISO 9000, will, having obtained registration, regard the quality issue as solved. With the exception of activities required to maintain the system (eg internal audits, record keeping etc) the managers will move on to other issues or 'get back to normal'. Such organisations miss the point. ISO 9000 is not an end in itself but rather part of a culture of continuous improvement.

In this final chapter, we introduce some additional quality management techniques. These are, in one way or another, extensions to activities described in previous chapters as requirements of ISO 9000.

THE STAGES OF QUALITY MANAGEMENT

Historically, quality management has moved through four stages; inspection, quality control, quality assurance and total quality management, or TQM. Each has built on the previous stage and at least up to quality assurance has largely incorporated the preceding technique into an enlarged discipline. For example, as we have discussed and will again shortly, inspection has its limitations but in practice, it is an integral part of quality assurance and a requirement of ISO 9000 – the standard for quality assurance.

It is difficult to imagine a commitment to quality management which did not include some element of inspection and rightly so. In certain industries – eg pharmaceuticals – a defined level of inspection is a regulatory requirement. However, problems arise when inspection is the sole or even main approach to quality management. In this case the firm cannot overcome some of its intrinsic limitations and can mistake busy work for a real attempt at quality improvement. In Chapter 2 we discussed some of these problems of inspection and particularly that the causes of rejected products may never be dealt with – waste is institutionalised – and that some qualities, particularly in the case of service businesses, simply cannot be checked in this way. However, there is another difficulty with inspection which is best explained by a simple example.

Turn back to the specimen quality policy on page 111 and count the number of the letter 'f's in it – perhaps it is an aim of Ashton-Jackson to put out only f-less literature. Allow an inspection period of 30 seconds and persuade someone else to do it as well. How many did you find and was this the same as the result from your co-inspector? Were you, or either of you, correct? The answer is in footnote 1 – at least that is our estimate although who is to say that we are right. So this is another problem with inspection. It is difficult and hard to arrive at 'true' rejection rates. Faced with these difficulties the dedicated inspection company may re-train its inspectors, get new ones in or double their number – all expensive routes to quality management and which still do not solve the problem of the faulty literature coming out of the typographical department. Also the human relations side of things will not be so good with a deep and suspicious divide between authors and the f-gestapo.

This moves us on to the next stage of quality management – quality control. In the example we perhaps go into the typographical department and see if we can find a solution in the process so that only f-less literature will in future come out of Ashton-Jackson. Simple – we can disable the f-key on the word processors! Quality control, therefore, involves supplementing an inspection regime by starting an 'analyse and prevent' culture. Usually though, quality control activities focus on only really serious problems – usually identified in inspection – and restrict the analysis to one part of the operation; production. Problems arising from such as faulty deliveries, the approach taken in purchasing, relations with customers, design work and so on are usually left outside the scope of a quality control approach.

The limitations of both inspection and quality control are overcome by a quality assurance approach with, as described in Chapter 2, a commitment to finding 'best ways' for all processes with any direct bearing on the final quality. Inspection elements are retained but restricted to where they must be used and often the need for them is reduced as problems are solved at source. Quality assurance of course brings into quality management ISO 9000 since this is the standard for effective quality assurance.

Quality assurance and ISO 9000 is about meeting requirements and solving the problems that get in the way of this goal. Arguably, the next step is not to just put things right (re-active) but to anticipate (pre-active). Not only to meet requirements but go beyond them. Now the question is not 'what needs fixing' but 'why is it not perfect' and quality improvement becomes the passion of the whole company. An ISO 9000 quality system at least partly concerns such 'super-quality' management – an effective system, as we have argued, builds in a dynamic of problem solving and improvement. However, the subtle but important change in the quality focus goes beyond ISO 9000 and moves us into the fourth stage of quality management – TQM. At least two of the case study companies – P&O European Ferries and DHL International – regard themselves as involved in a wider TQM approach as well as having effective quality systems in place.

In contrast to quality assurance and ISO 9000, TQM is a much less precise concept and rather than being a defined system it covers a range of techniques and cultures which various authors and gurus stress to a greater or lesser extent. One common theme is the involvement of all staff – not just so that such as a quality system works (unwilling and uninvolved staff will make sure that it does not) but because people, at all levels,

---

[1] We say there are 17 f's in the policy.

are seen as the only real source of quality improvement. Now all barriers to quality issues are dissolved and everything becomes part of the drive for quality. This is risky stuff of course. Once employees are truly empowered who can be sure where things will lead, and fearing this managements often use the term (but not the substance of) TQM as no more than a way of sugaring changes *they* know are right. After all the alternative is chaos. But as somebody[2] has said, there is no avoiding this and we must all learn to thrive on it.

This is all very well but what do you actually *do* in TQM programmes once the high sounding words have been spoken? Even a summary of the techniques and practices on offer from TQM is beyond the scope of this book but there are many excellent titles in the field – some suggestions are given in the bibliography. However, there are a number of TQM type activities which are really extensions of what is required for ISO 9000 and we shall conclude by briefly mentioning some of these.

GETTING CLOSER TO CUSTOMERS

ISO 9000 is based on meeting customer requirements and a heading of the Standard – *4.3 contract review* – specifies steps an organisation must take to ensure that these needs are understood and met. The concern, however, is primarily particular – each product, service and delivery, therefore, tends to fragment satisfying customers into meeting separate contracts. But customers do not often see a supplier relationship in this way. Rather they view it is a totality and on-going. A particular delivery may be perfect but the customer still not really delighted with the supplier. An extension to contract review can, therefore, be a far more open-ended and wide ranging approach to customers. This can involve asking questions such as 'What could we do better?', 'Should we do things differently?' and 'What can we do for you in future?' This approach can involve a major shift in the perspective of a

---

[2]   Tom Peters – see *Thriving On Chaos*.

company (and not just of the sales force) and if meaningful answers are found to the questions, this can lead to quality improvement teams producing a clear competitive advantage for the firm. However, getting the answers is not that easy even when only a few customers are involved. If a large and fragmented market is served, professional (ie from a market research company) assistance will very likely be needed.

Dealing with complaints is also a requirement of ISO 9000 with an emphasis on identifying root causes and long term solutions – not just making customers less unhappy but preventing the same thing happening again. However, complaints are often only made once problems have crossed some sort of threshold but before this level, satisfaction may be less than complete. If this sub-optimal satisfaction persists, some problems which could be put right, are neglected – until a 'last straw' leads to a real complaint, by which time the customer may be so dissatisfied that the business is lost. This may point to the need for a more pro-active approach to establishing customer satisfaction.

At its simplest, customer satisfaction monitoring need be no more than a short postal questionnaire, mailed to each customer (or a random sample if there are many) requesting a score (say from 1 – abysmal – to 10 – unsurpassable) to describe satisfaction with the overall service or various components of it (eg product design, manufacturing quality, keeping to delivery schedules etc). The results from customers can be averaged and goals set to improve the ratings over time (eg to have scores of 8 or more from 90 per cent of customers). Improvement in satisfaction, therefore, becomes something that is measurable. Moreover, the response can be a way of identifying latent complaints – eg any score of 7 or less on a 10 point scale is regarded as a customer complaint and investigated (possibly using a full corrective and preventive action approach). In this way, problems can be caught before they pass the customer's threshold of taking action against you, the supplier. Such customer satisfaction monitoring has become far more common in the last few years but it is still surprising that not more companies use the technique. 'Not bothering customers' is often trotted out as the excuse but this is ridiculous. Nearly everyone likes responding to such surveys because it relates to something very important; receiving good service. And at least it shows a commitment to customers – we care enough to value your opinion.

A final aspect of customer satisfaction to mention is the concept of 'internal customers'. It is all very well talking about satisfying customers, but in most companies, the majority of staff never get to meet a live customer. By engendering the view that each part of an organisation is both a supplier to and a customer of other departments, meeting requirements – quality – becomes a concern of everyone.

WORKING WITH SUPPLIERS

As much as what is done within the business, quality depends on what comes in – on purchasing. ISO 9000 has a requirement for purchasing systems (4.6) and three sub-headings within this. One of these is *4.6.2 – evaluation of subcontractors* (ie of suppliers). Meeting this involves, among other things, collecting and keeping records of suppliers' performance. However, little or nothing is required in terms of getting real benefits from all this data and there is a danger of it all becoming ISO 9000 paperwork – filled in meticulously, but to little purpose. It would make little commercial sense, but data showing that a supplier performed consistently badly, over a long time, could be adequate in relation to meeting the Standard.

The problem is that valuable data is often just not used effectively but with no extra work in record keeping, the data could form the basis of a really effective system of supplier appraisal. There are various established techniques of this sort to choose from. One approach is to collect supplier records together and review them periodically. It is then only a short step to categorise those where faults were apparent into sub-groups and thereby identify the most frequent areas of difficulty. These could, in turn, drive improvement teams working with the supplier's management to find a lasting solution. This is an example of using the purchasing system, not as stick to beat suppliers, but as a tool in working together.

Moving to more sophisticated systems (and probably a different type of record being kept), each delivery could be given a numerical score dependent upon the degree of conformance to the specification. Various aspects (eg dimensional accuracy, packaging, delivery timescale etc) could be included in the scoring and make up the overall total – perhaps weighted to allow for more or less important elements. With each delivery scored, it is possible to draw up a table of suppliers' performance, averaged out over a period (say three months). Once done, this would enable a company to direct its attention to those at the bottom of the league table; either to work with them to improve their performance or to find alternative sources of supply. In the same way, deliveries from suppliers at the head of the table could qualify for reduced levels of inspection (because of increased confidence in their product) with consequent savings of resources. Also suppliers could be offered incentives to encourage them to work towards rising to the top of the list – they might be allowed to use their customer's name in advertising, qualify for advantageous financial considerations such as quicker payment and so on. A common feature here is feedback; suppliers are more likely to improve if told of problems (the mirror of customer satisfaction monitoring). In Chapter 2 we mentioned how Datac Adhesives use a scoring system in this way.

The list of things that can be done in the purchasing area is endless once the information system has been created to support it. The bones of the system are usually already in place as a result of ISO 9000 and all that is required is the desire to use this data to real effect.

DEVELOPING PEOPLE

All organisations are as good as the people they employ. Service business companies generally recognise this but even a capital intensive manufacturing plant depends on its staff's skills. Unlike machinery, people can always improve no matter what their base level of skill.

ISO 9000 recognises this area under the heading *4.18 – training*. The requirement here does imply that training should be carried out but there is at least an equal stress, if not more, on identification of needs. Possibly the letter if not the spirit of the Standard would be met by a manager simply keeping a list of all staff and once a year writing against each name 'no training needed' – after the most careful consideration, of course. But even if this does meet an ISO 9000 assessment, nothing will be achieved quality-wise. An organisation which is serious about improvement must be committed to staff training and devote resources (especially management time) to it. Even the concept of training is a bit limited since it implies qualifying staff to carry out today's tasks. What about tomorrow's (as yet unknown) skills? This expands training to staff development. Again, this is a whole discipline of its own that we cannot develop here. A good start is contact with a local TEC. One of the initiatives taken up by TECs is the Investor In People standard, and working towards this may be worth considering (if you have not had enough of assessments by now). If nothing else, it is a framework around which to plan a staff development programme.

WORKING WITH NUMBERS

The requirement for using statistical methods has always seemed a bit uncomfortable in ISO 9000, even half hearted. In the 1994 revision the requirement was stressed a bit more (ie procedures for using statistics) but there still remains a let out. Having reviewed the situation, many companies can probably defend a view that they cannot identify any useful role for such techniques in their business. At bottom this may be valid but more often it is a fear that it will all be beyond them without hiring a PhD level statistician. This is a pity because some simple but powerful tools for quality improvement can be neglected – 'If you cannot measure it you cannot manage it' has some validity.

Perhaps it is best to talk of using numbers rather than statistics. A very simple example can illustrate some of the potential benefits that quantification of problems can bring. Consider the case of an organisation trying to improve (say by 10 per cent) the time it takes from the start of the first operation until the end of the last one. The process involved could be as indicated in Figure 12.1. It could be any process, manufacturing (such as assembling a motor) or a service (such as processing an order).

Each sub-process – A to D – plays a part in the overall activity, carrying out their allocated tasks and taking time to do it. When facing the problem of improving the overall time of the process, many would use 'common sense' and their knowledge of the tasks involved to decide that the thing to do is to add extra resource (more staff, a new computer etc) to say area B and that is that; end of problem. This may sound simplistic but it is used all too often, especially where there are vested interests to be served, eg the manager of area B *wants* a new computer.

However, without any knowledge about what the previous situation was, how can the new proposal be evaluated after it has been carried out? Better perhaps not to jump at a solution yet but to gather some information. This could be done by measuring the performance of each part over a period of time. Suppose the results shown in Figure 12.2 were obtained.

This now shows the area and transfer times, and by summing them together, an overall process taking 18 hours. Area B does seem to be the largest consumer of time so perhaps the new computer is the right answer after all. Suppose further investigation indicated that the computer would cost £10,000 and would reduce the time by one hour. Good news for manager B? An alternative approach, however, relates to transfer times. This takes up six hours, a third of the whole process time and larger than of any one area. Investigations indicate that re-organising transfer, (which would have zero cost) can save three hours. Such a solution could be implemented quickly and the improvement

Figure 12.1 Process flow

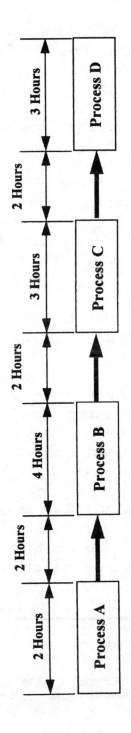

Figure 12.2 Process flow, with information

demonstrated. If it works then the target has been met. If not then other ideas could be tested in a similar way.

None of this could be regarded as high level mathematics and need not carry the frightening label of 'statistics'. Yet this approach, simplistic though it is, is based upon an actual case which yielded significant benefits for the company involved to the delight of all (except manager B).

Beyond this, further and more truly statistical techniques exist which need not be significantly more difficult. Many can be carried out using computer software, removing one of the reasons (difficult calculation) for avoiding them.[3] Some such techniques are based upon the concept of variation. Everything in the universe varies; no two things are identical. If this page were to be measured at six points, randomly selected, there would be six different measurements taken. Despite this variation, the printer has been able to produce a book that has passed through all the required printing processes. The question is, therefore, how much variation should be allowed before some action needs to be taken? If the variation in the paper became wider and wider, a point would be reached when the printing process would become affected, and ultimately prevented. The relevant statistical techniques are aimed at discovering what the normal (common) variability of a process is, and then using that data to identify if any other (special) variations, beyond the expected level, have occurred. Relevant action can then be considered. Figures 12.3 and 12.4 illustrate this.

Figure 12.3 shows a series of readings taken from a process over a period of time. As can be seen, the readings vary. However, the range of normal variation is not known and so it cannot be determined which, if any, of the points are outside this range. Any attempt to adjust this process, based upon this chart alone, is like shooting in the dark, and could actually make matters worse through adding yet another cause of variation.

---

[3] Beware though. What is important is that the results of any statistical analysis are *understood*. Button pushing is not a substitute for thinking.

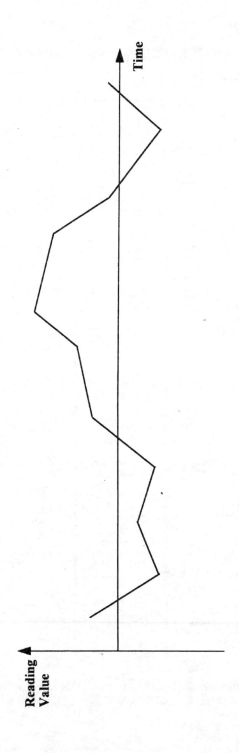

Figure 12.3 Process readings

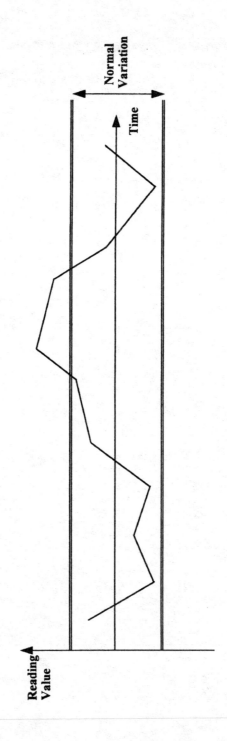

Figure 12.4 Process readings with range of variation

Now the same chart and readings are plotted, but together with an indication of the normal variation of the process. Anything outside this range is the result of some other, special, feature which should be tracked down and possibly eliminated. Causes of the effect could be anything from a change of the ingredient batch to a shift changeover. The chart indicates when the change occurred and what effect it had on the process. Since the process returned to within the normal range without alteration then perhaps the effect of the special change was a short one and this may help to assist in identifying the cause of the problem.

This can only be the briefest of introductions to statistical analysis but it will hopefully stimulate interest. As with other aspects of TQM, there are excellent books on the subject which explain both applications and how to do the analysis required.

REMAKING THE OMELETTE

Finally there is going back to basics and starting again. This is not directly linked to any specific requirement of ISO 9000 but rather to one of our suggestions for designing a system. By and large we recommended the existing practices should be changed as little as possible when developing a quality system. We think this is good advice but only in the context of a short term goal of achieving the Standard. Beyond this narrow perspective, this may be very poor advice indeed.

The processes and structures (departments, the hierarchy etc) of almost all organisations, at best represent the solutions to yesterday's challenges and at worst are no more than fossilised past mistakes. In an ever-changing world how we do things will increasingly have to be re-thought and periodically the need may be to start with a clean sheet and plan how the goals, whatever they are (they must include customers' needs), can best be met regardless of the existing arrangements. This is the re-engineering approach. No sensible manager will embark on this on a whim and without exploring the whole concept in some detail.

However, there are two key considerations in the approach we can mention here. The first is that it is essential to know what goal you are re-engineering for – if you have lost the destination, there is no point running harder. And nor is it always that obvious what an organisation's goal should be, and deep, clear thought may be essential. A photocopier supplier may think that failure-free machines and good back-up service is what customers require but in reality customers just want to produce copies when they need them and there may be better ways for the supplier to offer this. A broad vision and lateral thinking must, therefore, come first in any radical re-structuring. The second point to consider is that compared to our predecessors we are not supermen; there is no real evidence that we are all getting cleverer. Mistakes may have been made in the past but why will we do fundamentally better? However well planned, the re-engineered organisation will also soon be less than perfect.

YOU DO NOT HAVE TO DO THIS

These then are some ways of taking ISO 9000 further. We can only give a flavour and we urge you not to try any of them without learning more about quality management and its techniques. However, we have hopefully demonstrated that ISO 9000 should only be part of a longer-term process of change and improvement. It may all seem alarming and there is much to be said for taking things a step at a time. Get an ISO 9000 system up and running – done properly it is a very effective start – but in general, inactivity is no longer an option. As the quality expert Edward Deming has succinctly expressed it:

You do not have to do this. Survival is not compulsory.

Bibliography

Asher, JM (1992) *Implementing TQM in Small and Medium Sized Companies,* Technical Communications, Letchworth.

Dale, B and Oakland, JS (1991) *Quality Improvement Through Standards,* Stanley Thornes, Leckhampton.

Jackson, P and Ashton, D (1993) *Implementing Quality Through BS 5750 (ISO 9000),* Kogan Page, London.

Oakland, J (1989) *Total Quality Management,* Butterworth-Heinemann, Oxford.

Peters, T (1989) *Thriving on Chaos,* Pan Books, London.

Price, F (1984) *Right First Time,* Wildwood House, Aldershot.

Warwood, SJ (1993) *Role of the Modern Quality Manager,* Technical Communications, Letchworth.

Index

layout 105
legal requirements 82
Lloyds 28, 159
local government 25
loose leaf binder 105

mailshots 167
maintenance 65
management 22
management consultancy 60, 72
management of change 39
management representative 86, 94, 120, 138, 141, 142, 145
management responsibility 85, 86
management review 87, 94, 150
manufacturing 45, 82
marketing
  advantages 35
  benefits 33, 34
  gains 38
  tool 166
medical practices 25
meeting all requirements 16
Metropolitan Police 26
misconceptions 26
models 49
monitoring 39
morale 29

National Vocational Qualifications (NVQ) 80
non-conformity 141

NQA 28, 159

obsolete documents 90
on-site assessment 163
on-site business 161
operating process 53
opportunity costs 45
oppressive tool 33
organisation 87
organisational and technical interfaces 61
origins of ISO 9000 24
output 22
owners 16

P&O European ferries 14, 16, 17, 29, 31, 35, 36, 40, 69, 104, 162, 171
packaging 70
Park Farm 14, 36, 37, 42, 64, 81
performance of suppliers 76
pharmaceuticals 169
planning 22, 92
plating 117
pre-assessment 162
preparing for assessment 161
preservation 71
previous audits 143
problems 31
procedures 101, 117
  developing and drafting 131
  mandatory 103
process analysis 126, 128
process control 64, 65, 66, 71
process methods 36